The GREYHOUND

MARK SULLIVAN

BEST of BREED

ACKNOWLEDGEMENTS

The publishers would like to thank the following for help with photography: Graham Davies Photography, Steve Nash, Rita Bartlett (Ransley), Hanne Bockhaus (Eikica), Greyhounds in Need, Marcella Zapelli, Ele Rea at Meadowcroft Kennels (Hall Green Retired Greyhound Trust), Evesham Greyhound and Lurcher Rescue (Michelle Salter and Macy), Greyhound Rescue Wales – Alain Thomas, Kate and Andrew Woodhouse with Andy and Booty, Krista Collis with Poppy, Hearing Dogs for Deaf People, Pets As Therapy.

Special thanks to David Wolf and the National Greyhound Adoption Program and to Ivor Stocker and the Retired Greyhound Trust.

Cover photo: © Tracy Morgan Animal Photography (www.animalphotographer.co.uk)
Dog featured is Mistweave Me First, owned by Mr A & Mrs J Mackenzie.

Page 10 © istockphoto.com/Madjuska; page 11 © istockphoto.com/Dario Egidi;
Page 36 © istockphoto.com/Rick Szczechowski; page 122 © istockphoto.com/Tooties.

The British Breed Standard reproduced in Chapter 2 is the copyright of the Kennel Club and published with the club's kind permission. Extracts from the American Breed Standard are reproduced by kind permission of the American Kennel Club.

THE QUESTION OF GENDER
**The 'he' pronoun is used throughout this book instead of the rather
impersonal 'it', but no gender bias is intended**

First published in 2010 by The Pet Book Publishing Company Limited
Chepstow, NP16 7LG, UK.
Reprinted 2012.

ISBN
978-1-906305-39-0
1-906305-39-0

Printed and bound in China through Printworks International Ltd.

CONTENTS

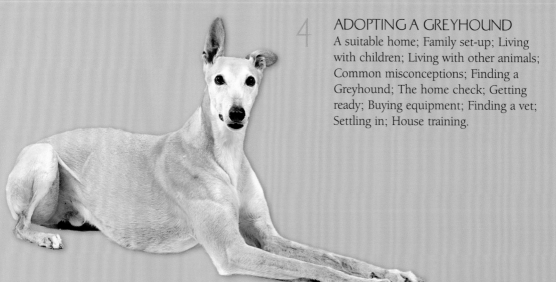

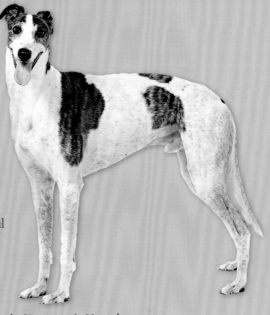

GETTING TO KNOW GREYHOUNDS

Chapter

1

W elcome to the Greyhound - a breed that can claim to be the most athletic in the world; one whose ancestry stretches back to almost the very beginning of time and whose elegance and charisma have made it one of the most pictured and written about in the canine kingdom.

There was a time when Greyhounds were so special that the aristocracy wanted them all for themselves. Thankfully, these days, everybody and anybody can indulge in the breed and they do so through an involvement in the racing, coursing, showing worlds, or by taking on a Greyhound that has retired from one of those sporting pursuits.

Many of you will have had Greyhounds for years and will be totally connected to the breed, some of you may have just recently adopted an ex-racing or coursing Greyhound and will be keen to learn more about your new best friend, while others might be contemplating taking on a Greyhound for the first time. If you fall into the latter category then take my advice – do it!

From a personal point of view, I became a fan of the breed as a youngster growing up in London in the Seventies. My family owned racing Greyhounds at the world famous White City stadium when, for the first time, we were confronted with the situation of retiring one of them from the track. We had a simple choice: either we could have him home as a pet or attempt to find a loving family for him to spend his retirement years.

We opted for the former and it was a decision we were never given cause to regret, as Happy, as he was known, was a complete joy. He settled into his new home with the professionalism he had showed throughout his racing career and was soon the life and soul of the place. He enjoyed good health and lived to a ripe old age, giving my family more fun and love than you could ever imagine – a lot more than we could possibly offer in return. From then on, my family was hooked on owning Greyhounds and at least one, sometimes more, has in the last four decades been ever-present in our home. I am pleased to say there is little likelihood that will ever change.

THE GREYHOUND FAMILY
The Greyhound is a member of the Sighthound family. Also known as gazehounds, this clan includes the likes of the Afghan Hound, the Basenji, the Deerhound, the Irish Wolfhound, the Pharaoh Hound, the Rhodesian Ridgeback, the Saluki,

THE GREYHOUND FAMILY

Rhodesian Ridgeback.

Irish Wolfhound.

Saluki.

Whippet.

Basenji.

the Sloughi, and the Whippet, among others.

The Sighthound, which gets its name because it hunts primarily by sight, can be traced back many thousands of years to the Middle East. Because of the vast, flat terrain of that region, a dog needed excellent eyesight to spot its prey and, given the expansive, open and extremely demanding territory, great speed, stamina and not least agility, to track it down for the kill. The Sighthound is entirely fit for that purpose.

Typically, the Sighthound carries little body fat. He is lean but also well muscled where it needs to be. The stamp of the family is long and sweeping,

angular, deep in chest and arched in back. Almost all Sighthounds have the trademark long, pointed head. There are exceptions, however, most notably the Basenji and the Rhodesian Ridgeback, both of whom are slightly thicker and stodgier in shape.

The Greyhound is the archetypal Sighthound. The animal is simply a template for pace and endurance. He is officially the fastest dog in the world with an ability to hit speeds of more than 40 mph (64 km per hour) over a distance of half a mile or 800 metres, if you prefer. Much of the leanness of the Greyhound can be attributed to a rapid metabolism, which

burns off fat cells quicker than that of any other breed and, courtesy of a responsible feeding and exercise regime, should ensure the dog maintains a healthy, athletic shape throughout his life. The Greyhound's construction includes an elongated snout, a long powerful neck, a beam of power for a back, and well-muscled hindquarters. All this is packaged in the most aerodynamic structure that proves whatever the likes of McLaren and Ferrari are spending fortunes on achieving on the race tracks of Formula 1, nature has the wherewithal to do just as well, if not better, and it doesn't cost a penny.

Afghan Hound.

Throughout its history (and there is evidence of a Greyhound-like creature walking the planet in 6,000BC) the Greyhound has been linked with hunting and sporting pursuits – whether it be chasing game with the pharaohs in Ancient Egypt, providing entertainment on the coursing fields for Queen Elizabeth I in the 1500s, or, right up to the present day, racing to success in the English Derby at Wimbledon Stadium in London.

All those pursuits involve channelled aggression, but it would be completely wrong to allow that to colour your perception of the Greyhound. Indeed, it is difficult to find a kinder, gentler and more courteous animal and it is those traits, allied to it being the most affectionate and loyal, that goes towards making the Greyhound the most perfect companion dog.

One of the earliest and most regularly quoted descriptions of the Greyhound can be found in the *Book of St Albans*, a collection of essays on hawking, hunting and heraldry, printed by St Albans Press in 1480. In it Dame Juliana Berners observes:

A Greyhound shold be
heeded lyke a snake
And neckyd lyke a drake,
Backed lyke a beam,
Syded lyke a bream,
Footed lyke a catte,
Taylld lyke a ratte

Today's Greyhound largely fits the identikit created by Berners. From a personal point of view, I like to see strong parallel limbs – cow hocks (hocks that point inward, causing the toes on the back feet to point outward) are often a sign of poor rearing and are a turn-off – and well-arched toes (sometimes referred to as boxed feet). Bright eyes and an intelligent head sit on a long, strong neck, maintaining the line from a broad, powerful back, supporting a deep chest and a tucked tummy. The male of the breed typically measures 28-30 inches (71-76 cms) to the shoulder and on average weighs anything between 65 lbs to 72 lbs (29-32 kilos). The females

The Greyhound was bred to chase, but he has the most gentle, endearing temperament.

The concept of Greyhounds racing around an oval track behind an artificial lure originated in the United Stakes and the first meeting there was staged at Emeryville in California in 1921. The UK had its first race around a track behind the mechanical bait at Belle Vue, Manchester, on 24 July 1926. The six-race programme drew a crowd of 1,700 who watched three contests over 440 yards, two over 500 yards and one hurdle contest over 440 yards. Greyhound racing in the UK was an instant hit, unlike in America where it took time to catch on.

The first Greyhounds to race on the track were drawn from coursing stock. But as track racing evolved through the generations, so did a breed of Greyhound produced specifically to race against five others around fixed bends. A mix of Irish and English coursing and track stock has, over the years, proven the most effective combination to produce in more recent times the best track performers. Greyhound breeders and trainers believe that the mix of those two strains brought something unique to the table.

The introduction of American and Australian blood in the late Seventies and Eighties had a positive initial impact on the UK track dogs. However, there is a school of thought that the retention of the Irish coursing strain in particular has been poor, and that, they say, has manifested in weaker-willed, less consistent Greyhounds. Certainly track

generally stretch the tape to 27-29 inches (68-71 cms) to the shoulder and tip the scales at anywhere between 60-65 lbs (27-29 kilos).

Most of you with Greyhounds in the home will have probably obtained your pet from one of the many organisations set up to find homes for former racing Greyhounds in either Australia, Ireland, the United Kingdom or the United States. These are the four main nations where Greyhound racing takes place on a professional footing. Greyhound racing is also conducted in many other countries around the world, including in mainland Europe and Scandinavia, where it is usually on a more "for fun" basis, which often means the racing

dogs are also the family pets and therefore remain as such when their racing days are over.

THE RACING AND COURSING GREYHOUND
Many people will have acquired their first experience of the Greyhound at their local racetrack. When racing at high speed, particularly in the evenings when the track lighting extenuates every muscle-stretching stride, the breed is *the* most aesthetically appealing and exciting animal to watch. Today's racing Greyhound in the UK is the product of years of careful breeding, using the best home bloodlines combined with the leading strains from Australia, Ireland and the United States.

The concept of racing Greyhounds round an oval track came from the USA.
Graham Davies Photography.

Greyhounds do not appear to be as resolute as they were 20 years ago. They are definitely quicker – the clock does not lie – although that could be, in part, attributed to better track preparation methods but that will-to-win they possessed in the past does not seem to be as evident these days.

Greyhounds start to race in the UK at 15 months. In Ireland they are allowed to begin their careers at 14 months. Injury permitting, a Greyhound can race into its sixth year, but it is more likely that he will retire from the race track at four to five years of age. Most racing Greyhounds in the UK will be attached to a track during their careers. That means they will be housed at the kennels of a trainer who is contracted to supply a set number of racers to one of the

current number of 27 tracks in the UK controlled by the Greyhound Board of Great Britain. The majority of these attached kennels will house between 60 to 80 Greyhounds. Their trainer – assisted by kennel staff – will prepare the Greyhounds, all of whom will be required to take part in a series of time trials to ascertain their ability and also that they are genuine chasers before they are allowed to race.

Racing Greyhounds are remarkably consistent animals. Week in week out, over a period of two or three years, the Greyhound will perform to within a 10th to a 20th of a second every time it races. Gamblers clearly admire the dependability of the Greyhound because more than £2 billion annually is

invested on racing in the UK alone.

The distances that Greyhounds race over are pretty much standard worldwide. In Britain and Ireland the majority of races – and most of the prestigious competitions – take place over distances between 480 metres and 550 metres around an oval track.

The shortest race under the rules of the Greyhound Board of Great Britain is a little over 200 metres and the longest distance is a just over 1,000 metres. The Derby, just as in horse racing, is the major race and in the UK it is staged over 480 metres. Greyhound racing also has its own Oaks and St Leger, which, like the Derby, are staged at Wimbledon.

Coursing was made illegal in

the UK in February 2005 on the introduction of the Labour Party's 2004 Hunting Bill, which outlawed hunting with dogs. In Ireland, however, the sport is still popular. The season runs from September to March and culminates with the National Meeting in February and the Irish Cup in March.

Size is the principal difference between the Irish coursing dog and track dog. The coursing dog is bigger. The average size of a male courser is around 84-86 lbs (38-39 kilos) while a female courser is approximately 76-78 lbs (35-36 kilos). It seems, however, this has come about more by chance than a desire to produce a dog that has superior pace in a straight line, which the larger dog does.

Matt Bruton, an authority on Irish breeding, who writes on the subject in *The Sporting Press*, reported:

"Up until the Sixties coursing Greyhounds were not significantly bigger than track dogs but then along came Newdown Heather.

"He was a very influential sire who not only put a lot of size into his progeny but was also responsible for introducing white as a dominant colour in the markings of the coursing greyhounds."

"From my experience, the temperament of an Irish coursing dog is also slightly different from his track counterpart. Those I have come into contact with have been less excitable and possibly even kinder with perhaps more manners."

Most coursing in Ireland is classed as Park Coursing and takes place in an enclosed field. The emphasis is on speed, as the two dogs competing are released by the slipper behind a hare, which is trained to run in a straight line from the shelter (the point of departure for the dogs) to the escape. The wearing of muzzles, specifically designed for coursing, is mandatory in Ireland and the winner of the course is the first Greyhound that causes the hare to 'turn' (to deviate its course).

Open coursing – the type of coursing that was most popular in the UK until its ban – requires more of the Greyhounds in terms of work rate. This takes place in open countryside. The hares are flushed out by beaters towards an

The show Greyhound is an impressive looking dog.

area where the slipper is waiting to release the Greyhounds. A judge, on horse back, will observe the course and he or she will award points to each of the Greyhounds, which are identified by wearing either a red or white collar, depending on how they work (turn) the hare. The winner is the Greyhound that is considered to have worked the hare harder. Unlike in Ireland, coursing Greyhounds in the UK were not required to wear muzzles.

THE SHOW DOG

Having grown up with racing Greyhounds, I admit to being a little taken aback when encountering for the first time Greyhounds that had been bred for the show ring. The show type is generally bigger than its track counterpart and perhaps even larger - imposing would be a better word – in a different way to the coursing dog

The show dog is taller than the track dog and has a larger bone structure. The feet of the show dog also caught my eye. They are very neat – in some cases more "cat-like" than "hare-like" (which counts as a fault in the show ring) and they are very upright in the toe and also in the pastern.

To my eye, the show dog is more elegant in appearance. He has a longer, more arched neck than the racing dog, less muscle, particularly in the shoulder area, has more dramatic, exaggerated lines, a greater arching back and a tail that is longer and sits lower. The show dog carries less muscle than the track dog and courser, because it is felt by exhibitors that bulk precludes smooth lines, as breeders of the show Greyhound endeavour to produce an animal that adheres to the Breed Standard, a blueprint produced by the Kennel Club describing how the "perfect Greyhound" should look.

To be acknowledged as a Champion, a show Greyhound must win three Challenge Certificates awarded by different judges at three Championship shows. That is at the sharp end of showing; however, as much fun and less pressure can be enjoyed participating in less formal Companion Shows and the slightly more serious Open Shows.

A former racing champion, Scotts has now found a new role.

Working as an assistance dog, Scotts is now helping children to improve their literacy skills.

WORKING IN OTHER FIELDS

Greyhounds, mostly those that have retired from racing, are proving marvellous ambassadors for the breed and extremely effective as therapy dogs. Pets As Therapy (PAT), a national registered charity in the UK, was launched in 1983 and since then it has registered more than 22,000 dogs of all breeds to visit hospitals, hospices, nursing and care homes, schools and an assortment of other venues throughout the UK, providing important therapy for those that need it.

Before qualifying to be active within the PAT scheme, all dogs and cats must undergo a temperament assessment, which establishes that the animal is sociable, friendly, calm and suitable for the work it will be required to undertake. Greyhounds are proving highly adept as therapy dogs, mainly because of their placid temperament, which means they are perfectly happy to be stroked and handled by people for whom interaction with animals can prove important and beneficial as part of their health-care programme.

Many of those that receive help from therapy dogs are either bed-ridden or in a wheelchair. In these cases the height of the Greyhound also comes in particularly handy because they can be reached without causing discomfort to the patient. The fact that Greyhounds do not shed nearly as much coat as some other breeds also makes them highly desirable for use anywhere where hygiene is of paramount importance.

Among those that benefit from meeting therapy dogs are the elderly, some of whom may have had to abandon animals of their own when they were placed into the health-care system or into sheltered accommodation. They can experience a great deal of distress when having to surrender their pets and Pets As Therapy has found that beneficial bonds can be established by bringing dogs into these centres where the patients come to look on them as their own.

Helping children to read is another area where Greyhounds

are proving useful, and Scotts is one Greyhound leading the way. Formerly known as Scotts Kelly on the track, where he was a champion, winning the prestigious Arc at Walthamstow in 2001, Scotts is proving as talented off the track as part of the Reading Education Assistance Dogs (READ) scheme. Reading Education Assistance Dogs are specially trained, registered therapy dogs that sit with children, and, through their presence, encourage them to enjoy reading. Research shows that children are often more willing to interact with an animal rather than a person.

The programme is in its infancy in the UK but is already extremely successful in the USA where children who participate in the programme are said to make enormous progress building their reading and communication skills, while also developing their confidence and self-esteem. The project is aimed at children aged

between four and seven at both mainstream and special-needs schools.

Education professionals in the UK say READ has already made a significant impact and Scotts and another former racer by the name of Batman are at the forefront of that. Tony Nevett, the owner of Scotts, said: "Many children find it a struggle to read and it really knocks their confidence if they stumble over words in front of their mates.

"The idea of reading to dogs is that they don't answer back and don't give children a hard time if they don't get it right first time." He continued: "Greyhounds are extremely docile. They are couch potatoes who get on well with children and like nothing better than to sit around getting fussed."

GIVING BLOOD

For a number of reasons Greyhounds are classed as extremely desirable donors when

it comes to giving to dog blood banks. In fact, veterinarians are so keen to collect their blood that they offer free worming and vaccinations in return for donations. So what is it about the Greyhound's blood that makes it so appealing?

Well, to start with, Greyhounds have a higher red blood cell count than other breeds and consequently have a higher pack cell volume, which puts great value on them as contributors of blood. Greyhounds have been described as universal blood donors, as it is thought that as much as 70 per cent of the breed has blood that can be used by any other type of dog. A spokesperson for one of the leading veterinary companies in the UK that runs a dog blood donor scheme said: "Greyhounds are fabulous donors. Dogs must be over 25 kilos to donate in the first place, so given some exceptions – obviously small bitches and extremely small dogs

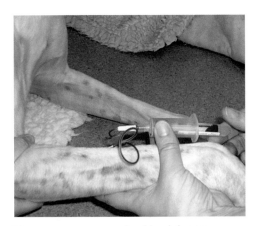

Many ex-racers are used as blood donors.

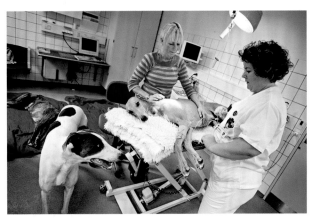

Photos courtesy: Hanne Bockhaus.

The Greyhound's easy-going temperament means that if his chase instinct is not too strong, he will socialise well with other animals.

– Greyhounds virtually always fit the bill."

The temperament of the Greyhound is also a consideration. "Most of the Greyhounds used for donating blood are ex-racers. They are used to being handled in the way necessary for taking blood and are therefore completely at ease when the process is underway.

"Also, because Greyhounds are such lean animals, it is easy to locate the jugular vein from which the blood is drawn. They are not frightened when needles are used because they are familiar with medical treatment, which they may experience during their racing days."

Blood is taken from any one Greyhound every three months and many Greyhounds become regular donors.

GETTING ON WITH OTHER ANIMALS

Greyhounds, by virtue of their easy-going nature, have an endearing ability to get on with other animals and in certain cases that sociability can be focussed on helping others.

A case in point is Jasmine, who since being rescued by the Nuneaton and Warwickshire Wildlife Sanctuary back in 2003, has been surrogate mother to more than 50 other animals.

"She dotes on the animals as if they were her own," said Geoff Grewcock, who runs the sanctuary. He added: "It's incredible to see. She takes all the stress out of them and it helps them to feel not only very close to her but to settle into their new surroundings."

Others that have been on the receiving end of Jasmine's kindness includes five fox cubs, four badger cubs, 15 chicks, eight guinea pigs, two stray puppies and, of all things, 15 rabbits.

What makes her kindness all the more special is that Jasmine hardly had the happiest of times in the past herself. She was found distressed and abandoned in a garden shed. She was nervous and in an emaciated condition and police, who took her to the sanctuary, believed she had been abused.

Geoff Grewcock said: "Having been neglected herself, to see her show so much affection to other creatures is a real surprise. But it is not just other animals, as she is also extremely close to children. She is such a gentle and big-hearted dog."

It is wrong to suggest that all Greyhounds are as considerate and giving with other animals as Jasmine clearly is but, nevertheless, Greyhounds are fairly good mixers and get on well with most other animals. But Greyhounds, like humans, are all different. Some will have no problem socialising and will mix well with other animals;

Bred to be the ultimate canine athlete, it is, in fact, the Greyhound's superb temperament that makes him so special.

others will prefer their own company. In extreme cases, some Greyhounds may be practically impossible to integrate with others.

It is always important to take the correct precautions when introducing a Greyhound for the first time to any other animal. Make sure the dog is muzzled and on a lead at all times. The meeting should be conducted on neutral territory.

GREYHOUNDS OVERCOMING DISABILITY

The Greyhound is a brave breed, as illustrated by the story of Elliot, who has overcome blindness to lead a full life.

Elliot has been blind since birth, but with help of his owners, Rick and Maxine Game, who obtained him from Cheryl Miller's rehoming kennels in Kent, he can do almost

everything a fully sighted Greyhound can. That includes walking up and down stairs and taking part in agility tests.

Animal lovers Rick and Maxine (who also own another Greyhound, Mr D'Arcy, two Miniature Dachshunds, Meg and Rheinhard, and Gianni the cat) have never let Elliot's disability stop him enjoying life. Indeed, Elliot has gone from strength to strength and is currently enrolled in agility and discipline classes at the Wagging Tails Dog School in South Norwood. Elliott can now respond to simple commands, such as: "careful", "right" and "left", which helps him to stay safe when he's out and about.

Rick explains: "Elliot is the most amazing pet and he brings smiles to our faces every day. We are so proud of the tremendous progress he has made – he's just

amazing and lives a very happy life in spite of his blindness."

"When we saw Elliot's picture on the Retired Greyhound Trust website and then saw Elliot, we fell in love with his sweet nature – with his white patches and grey mottling fur, Maxine and I knew we had found the Greyhound for us and a companion for our other pets, who simply adore him."

Cheryl said: "Elliot's story is extraordinary and we are delighted that he has flourished so well with Rick and Maxine. It goes to show that retired Greyhounds, even if they have flaws or disabilities, can still lead complete and fulfilling lives. Elliot's progress in his agility and his ability to respond to commands is truly inspiring."

Elliot's story is truly inspirational and whets the appetite for what is to follow.

THE PERFECT GREYHOUND

Chapter 2

How to define the perfect Greyhound? It's a topic as broad as it is long, and one to which there is no definitive answer. That was also the view of Dr John Walsh who, in the late 1800s, was charged with the responsibility of writing the first ever Breed Standard for the Greyhound. Walsh, who wrote under the pen name *Stonehenge*, had earlier observed in his 1853 book, The *Greyhound*, that there was no definitive Breed Standard, certainly not one from which it was possible to select the perfect specimen for breeding.

As somebody who cut his Greyhound teeth owning and handling track racers, I tend to side with Walsh, as it was the sheer diversity of type all filed under the heading 'Greyhound' that captured my imagination. From a track point of view, while

there are those that are, perhaps, easier on the eye than others, the final arbiter is the performance; the faster they race, the better they look. Aesthetic considerations are given short shrift in the racing world.

Track dogs come in all shapes and sizes, being the product of a mix from a myriad of racing strains from the Americas to Ireland and from Australia to the United Kingdom. Smaller, angular bitches were always perceived as having the best stamina; the heavier dog, broader on the shoulders and hindquarters, always seemed to possess superior early speed, and the taller, still well-muscled but ultimately more athletic type, seemed to excel in the more prestigious races between 480-700 metres. While that seems a rather general rule, it's uncanny how often it worked out that way.

WHAT IS A BREED STANDARD?

A Breed Standard does exist for the Greyhound. It describes how an ideal specimen of the breed looks, behaves and moves. Each Breed Standard contains a series of clauses with identical headings, which describe the various points of the breed.

The Breed Standard is determined as a result of consultation between the owners of a breed who get together to form a breed club, under the auspices of the Kennel Club. At the outset the Breed Standard is the subject of considerable discussion between the members of the breed club.

Once a degree of agreement has been reached, the format and content are submitted to the Kennel Club's Breed Standards sub-committee. Dialogue will then take place between the breed club and the Kennel Club

The Breed Standard is a written blueprint describing the 'perfect' Greyhound.
Photo: Sue Domun.

to refine the Breed Standard. Once the final version has been arrived at, it is presented to the Kennel Club's general committee for final approval.

Breed Standards may be reviewed at any time – clubs can submit proposed revisions, giving explanations as to why the amendments are considered necessary. Then, once again, discussion ensues and the general committee's final approval is required. The Kennel Club reviews all Breed Standards on a regular basis to ensure that the information given is consistent in its drive to promote healthy dogs and curb exaggerations. Most recently, a clause has been introduced to all British Breed Standards to ensure that a breed is "fit for purpose", meaning that it is, theoretically, still capable of carrying out the task it was originally bred for.

The Breed Standard for the Greyhound has been drawn and influenced by the show Greyhound, an animal that originates from the same gene pool as those that ply their trade on the track and/or up the field but one that, through time and selective breeding, has seen its racing appearance replaced by smoother lines and a softer, arguably more elegant, look.

All of which raises a problem for those Greyhounds from a track pedigree that also compete in the show ring. One Kennel

Club judge said: "Track dogs are at a disadvantage because the Breed Standard has been influenced by the show dog. Occasionally you will come across a dog that ticks all the right boxes but if he or she is opposed by a show dog, whose appearance will almost always be more in line with the Breed Standard, the show dog will always win."

It is the mission of the Breed Standard to highlight the elements of the Greyhound that separates it from other breeds. The Breed Standards I have used below are those from the UK Kennel Club (KC) and the American Kennel Club (AKC). Both are compiled following consultation with breed clubs in their respective countries. The Fédération Cynologique Internationale (FCI) is the governing body in Europe responsible for Breed Standards. The Standard issued by the FCI is the same as the breed's country of origin, which, in the Greyhound's case, is the UK.

ANALYSIS AND INTERPRETATION

GENERAL APPEARANCE

KC
Strongly built, upstanding, of generous proportions, muscular power and symmetrical formation, with long head and neck, clean well laid shoulders, deep chest, capacious body, slightly arched loin, powerful quarters, sound legs and feet,
and a suppleness of limb, which emphasise in a marked degree its distinctive type and quality.

That the Greyhound is one of the most imposing of breeds is perfectly captured in this appraisal from the Kennel Club. The symmetry of the breed and defined lines – two of its most outstanding features – are highlighted in this accurate pen portrait. The power, grace and dexterity are also underlined. The Greyhound's long head and neck are major contributory factors to the august stamp of the breed, while the deep chest and arched loin add to his impressive and proud physical presence. Overall,

the impression is of a dog that embodies robustness and powerfulness, while retaining an elegant posture and authority.

The American Kennel Club does not provide a summary of the general appearance of the Greyhound, or some of the other salient features, such as temperament and movement, although it does offer a scale of points, which brings into focus the more pertinent aspects of the breed's physical appearance.

CHARACTERISTICS

KC

Possessing remarkable stamina and endurance.

The Greyhound is strongly built, combining muscular power with symmetrical formation.
Photo courtesy Hanne Brockhaus.

The Greyhound is highly valued for his gentle, affectionate nature.

These observations lend more to the track Greyhound or coursing Greyhound and in that regard they are accurate. Given the nature of his work, they are not as discernable in the show Greyhound.

TEMPERAMENT

KC
Intelligent, gentle, affectionate and even-tempered.

Greyhounds mix fantastically with children and, given time and the right temperament, they will also get along with other animals, including cats. The breed is noted for its affection and also

devotion to its owner. It is rare for the Greyhound to exhibit a tendency to be aggressive or even bad-tempered, although some strains of the breed are prone to nervousness and also a little skittish.

HEAD AND SKULL

KC
Long, moderate width, flat skull, slight stop. Jaws powerful and well chiselled.

AKC
Long and narrow, fairly wide between the ears, scarcely perceptible stop, little or no development of nasal sinuses,
good length of muzzle, which should be powerful without coarseness.

The elongated nose – in common with the general streamlined and aerodynamic stamp of the breed – is one of the most distinctive features of the Greyhound, although it is not a major judging point. The skull is flat but the general appearance of the head is domed, exuding an air of intelligence.

EYES

KC
Bright, intelligent, oval and obliquely set. Preferably dark.

The nose is elongated and the eyes are obliquely set.

When a Greyhound is alert, the ears are semi-pricked.
Photo: Sue Domun.

AKC
Dark, bright, intelligent, indicating spirit.

The view among some Greyhound breeders and owners is that light or staring eyes can sometimes be an indication of dishonesty. Darker eyes are said to be a sign of the Greyhound being of an honest and genuine nature. A darker eye also gives off a kinder demeanour. Puppies born with slightly light eyes may develop darker eyes later in life.

EARS

KC
Small, rose-shape, of fine texture.

AKC
Small and fine in texture, thrown back and folded, except when excited, when they are semi-pricked.

Although appealing in appearance, rigid, upright ears are looked upon unfavourably. Ears are generally folded, but triangular in shape when they are opened out.

MOUTH

KC
Jaws strong with a perfect, regular and complete scissor bite, i.e. the upper teeth closely overlapping lower teeth and set

square to the jaws.

AKC
Teeth very strong and even in front.

The jaws should be strong and even. Teeth should be level. Overshot and undershot jaw is a definite fault.

NECK

KC
Long and muscular, elegantly arched, well let into shoulders.

AKC
Long, muscular, without

Shoulders must be set back to allow for a low-reaching gait.
Photo: Sue Domun.

throatiness, slightly arched, and widening gradually into the shoulder.

I have always considered the neck to be one of the breed signatures. It should be long but also powerful and supple to do the job for which it was intended – providing the leverage to lift the captured quarry from the ground. It is obviously important that the length of the neck marries to the body of the hound – otherwise balance is compromised – and the dog's line is maintained from the base of the ears until the neck meets the shoulders.

FOREQUARTERS

KC
Shoulders oblique, well set back, muscular without being loaded, narrow and cleanly defined at top. Forelegs, long and straight, bone of good substance and quality. Elbows free and well set under shoulders. Pasterns of moderate length, slightly sprung. Elbows, pasterns and toes inclining neither in nor out.

AKC
Shoulders: Placed as obliquely as possible, muscular without being loaded.
Forelegs: Perfectly straight, set well into the shoulders, neither turned in nor out, pasterns strong.

The preference is for oblique shoulders that are well set back to permit the desired extended and low gait. Shoulders should be muscled but not too heavy. The shoulder blades ought to slope towards each other from the top but there should be a big enough gap between the blades to prevent them from touching when the dog's head is lowered to the ground.

The forelegs should be straight and long, but relative to the rest of the dog's body, and the bone of good quality. If the engine of the dog is the hindquarters, the balance is primarily the job of the forelegs. These must be strong to carry the weight of the dog but muscle should be unobtrusive. A free moving elbow – ideally set below the shoulder blade – is important for a suitable gait. The pasterns are expected to be well sprung, of a moderate length and straight.

BODY

KC

Chest deep and capacious, providing adequate heart room. Ribs deep, well sprung and carried well back. Flanks well cut up. Back rather long, broad and square. Loins powerful, slightly arched.

AKC

Chest: Deep, and as wide as consistent with speed, fairly well-sprung ribs.
Back: Muscular and broad.
Loins: Good depth of muscle, well arched, well cut up in the flanks.

A deep chest is the hallmark of the breed – it should be noted that the track-bred dog's chest is not nearly as spacious as that of the show dog – and the Breed Standard demands that the chest falls to the level of the elbow. The ribs ought to be well sprung – without encroaching on the elbows and consequently the gait of the dog – to provide accommodation for a large heart and lungs.

The tucked-up tummy gives the dog his shape. Heavier dogs will carry a bit of a paunch, which would corrupt the smooth lines. The back should be long, broad and powerful as it holds the whole thing together. The trademark arc of the back should umbrella the loin area and should not be the complete length of the back.

HINDQUARTERS

KC

Thighs and second thighs wide and muscular, showing great propelling power. Stifles well bent. Hocks well let down, inclining neither in nor out. Body and hindquarters, features of ample proportions and well coupled, enabling adequate ground to be covered when standing.

AKC

Long, very muscular and powerful, wide and well let down, well-bent stifles. Hocks well bent and rather close to ground, wide but straight fore and aft.

This is the powerhouse of the Greyhound and aesthetically comparable with any breed. The width and depth of the muscle should be perfectly symmetrical when viewed from the rear and should run down to short hocks, which are expected to be vertical and have no bias even inward or outward. The stifle (the canine equivalent of the knee) should be well bent, and the upright hocks accommodate well-sprung toes.

FEET

KC

Moderate length, with compact, well knuckled toes and strong pads.

The chest must be deep and wide to provide adequate heart room.
Photo: Rita Bartlett.

The Greyhound moves with a low-reaching free stride.
Photo Courtesy: Hanne Bockhaus.

AKC

Hard and close, rather more hare than cat feet, well knuckled up with good strong claws.

Well-knuckled and strong feet are another of the Greyhound's outstanding features. The American Standard calls for a Greyhound to have "hare feet" (the two centre toes are longer than those that flank either side) as opposed "cat feet" (more compact with a shorter third digit). Feet should be flat and not splayed (often a sign of poor rearing), and pads should be substantial and strong. Nails, which are expected to be strong and healthy, should be kept neatly trimmed.

TAIL

KC

Long, set on rather low, strong at root, tapering to point, carried low, slightly curved.

AKC

Long, fine and tapering with a slight upward curve.

The tail should be long, set low, solidly set at the root, slightly curved and tapering. The length of the tail is important, as it acts as a rudder when the Greyhound is running. A shorter tail is less effective and should therefore be considered a fault.

GAIT/MOVEMENT

KC

Straight, low-reaching, free stride enabling the ground to be covered at great speed. Hind legs coming well under body giving great propulsion.

Free-flowing, straight and low-reaching. Hind legs should get right under the body of the dog for increased uplift and propulsion in order to achieve the greater speed that is required by the Breed Standard.

COAT

KC

Fine and close.

AKC

Short, smooth and firm in texture.

The coat of a Greyhound should be smooth and very short. When well maintained and groomed regularly, the coat will be silky to the touch and gleaming to the eye.

COLOUR

KC

Black, white, red, blue, fawn, fallow, brindle or any of these colours broken with white.

AKC

Immaterial.

The American Kennel Club has a very casual approach, stating that the colour is immaterial. The

GREYHOUND COLOURS

The Greyhound comes in a full range of colours.

Brindle and white.

Fawn.

Blue with white markings.

Black with white markings.

Black and white.

White and Brindle.

Kennel Club is more specific, stating all the recognised colours: black, white, red, blue, fawn, yellow (possibly also known as buff), brindle or any of these broken with white.

SIZE

KC
Ideal height: dogs: 71-76 cms (28-30 ins); bitches: 69-71 cms (27-28 ins).

AKC
Weight: Dogs, 65 to 70 pounds; bitches 60 to 65 pounds.

Generally, the categories in the Breed Standard are pretty comprehensively covered in their detail, but both the Kennel Club and American Kennel Club are less clear when it comes to size and weight. The Kennel Club makes no reference to weight, while the American Kennel Club has ignored height, so it is difficult to reconcile their respective observations. A 65-lb (29-kg) dog, as described in the American Breed Standard, would not be my favourite to catch the eye of the show ring judge, neither would a larger 30-inch (76-cm) to the shoulder dog as observed in the UK Standard, weighing in at a paltry 65 lbs. Certainly, in terms of weight, there seems to have been a gross underestimation.

The judge must assess each Greyhound and, according to his interpretation, decide which dog conforms most closely to the Breed Standard.
Photo: Hanne Bockhaus.

FAULTS

KC
Any departure from the foregoing points should be considered a fault and the seriousness with which the fault should be regarded should be in exact proportion to its degree and its effect upon the health and welfare of the dog.

Note: Male animals should have two apparently normal testicles fully descended into the scrotum.

The degree to which a dog adheres or does not adhere to the Breed Standard is pretty much at the discretion of the acting judge.

SCALE OF POINTS

AKC

General Symmetry and Quality	10
Head and Neck	20
Chest and Shoulders	20
Back	10
Quarters	20
Legs and Feet	20
Total	100

THE FIRST GREYHOUNDS

Chapter 3

Evidence from drawings discovered in the ancient Turkish town of Catal-Huyuk, placing a Greyhound-like dog there more than 8,000 years ago, is the foundation to the belief that the Greyhound family is probably the earliest purebred dog in existence. Excavated from the city located in the south-west of Turkey, the drawings are believed to date back as far as 6000BC. They depict an animal with the stellar characteristics of the Greyhound – a long head and supple neck, long legs and deep chest, and extended and powerful hindquarters – assisting in the slaying of a stag.

Further early proof of the existence of a Greyhound family is provided by the discovery of a funerary vase in what is now south-west Iran – with images of what appear to be Greyhound depicted on it – dating back to

4200BC. Sketches have also been discovered that puts a Greyhound-like dog in the Algerian Sahara area at about 3000BC and from there, over the following five centuries, it is believed the breed made its way to Egypt.

The term 'Greyhound family', while all-embracing, is probably the most accurate description of the animal that appears in the early images, as there is no clear corroborative proof that it was indeed the Greyhound. However, it is similar enough for us to believe it is a genuine forerunner of the modern Greyhound.

The Egyptians loved their dogs regardless of the breed. The killing of a canine was punishable by death and when favourite dogs passed away they were mummified and buried in a canine cemetery. The ancient Egyptians were instantly drawn to the Greyhound and quickly the

breed became the most coveted of them all. Being great hunters, the Egyptian noblemen were in awe of the sheer physicality of the breed. Its speed and instinct to chase made the Greyhound a very willing and valued partner in the pursuit of game.

The method of hunting in Ancient Egypt was perhaps the prototype of modern-day coursing. Two Greyhounds were released to chase, bring down and kill their prey, which included antelopes, hares, gazelles, stags and ostriches. Given their status in Egyptian society, the gift of a Greyhound was seen as suitable for the most important overseas visitors. Greyhounds were also used to barter for goods and services, and it was through that activity that the Greyhound began to make its way out of the Middle East and travel further afield.

The Greyhound found its way

The Greyhound is featured in Greek mythology.

to Ancient Greece around 1000BC and the locals welcomed the breed in much the same enthusiastic way as the Egyptians had done. The Greeks were great admirers of the Greyhound's form and it is depicted in much of the art of the period, including assisting in the hunt, at the feet of a master, and at play. They appreciated the fine lines of the breed and made good use of them in many everyday scenes. Indeed, the Greyhound is even featured on some of the coins from the period.

Homer, the Greek poet, gives the Greyhound what is believed to be its first mention in literature when, in 800BC, considering the return of Odysseus in *The Odyssey* and how Argos, his Greyhound, was the only one to recognise his returning master after a 20-year absence.

The Greyhound would later be the first breed mentioned in English written literature – up until then all manuscripts were written in French or Latin – when, in the late 14th century, Chaucer wrote in *The Canterbury Tales:*

Greyhounds he hadde as swift as fowels in flight;
Of priking and hunting for the hare
Was al his lust, for no cost wolde he spare

Still on a literary theme, the Greyhound is most famously the only dog mentioned in the Bible. In Proverbs 30, verses 29-31 it says:

There be three things which go well, yea,
Which are comely in going:
A lion, which is strongest among beasts and turneth not away from any;
A Greyhound: A he-goat also.

34

MYTH AND LEGEND

In addition to being the subject of fascination and adoration from the artisans of the era, the Greeks also used the Greyhound for the primary purpose of hunting and it was also in demand as a companion dog.

In Greek mythology, Hecate, the goddess of wealth, is rarely depicted without at least one Greyhound by her side. And it was as a companion dog to Alexander the Great, the King of Macedonia and leader of the Greeks, that a Greyhound by the name of Peritas is believed to have changed the course of history.

Legend has it that when his master was under siege from troops representing Persia's Darius III in 333BC, Peritas leapt at an elephant that appeared to be charging towards Alexander the Great, biting its lip and bringing the wanton animal to an abrupt halt. Sadly, Peritas is believed to have died during that battle. His master was so in awe of his dog's bravery and so indebted to the animal for saving his life that he organised a state funeral for the hound and even named a city in its honour.

Alexander went on to win the battle and to create an empire that sprawled three continents, covering approximately two million square miles, and thus laying the foundations for Western civilisation.

THE ROMAN ERA

Like the Greeks, the Romans had a fondness for dogs that went

NAMING THE BREED

There has been, and still is to this day, conjecture over the origin of the name 'Greyhound'. One theory is that the name is derived from the term Greek Hound and was acquired during the Ancient Greek period of the dog's evolution. Other theories say it comes from 'grech' or 'greg', the old English word for 'dog'. One school of thought that does not hold much water, however, is that the name relates to the colour grey. The reason for the incredulity is that Greyhounds have never been grey in colour as far as we know; the closest they come is the blue colour that is currently quite dominant among racing stock in the UK today, and much of that has originated from the use of Australian sires.

further than viewing them just as a tool for hunting. The Greyhound was instantly popular with the genteel side of Roman society when it arrived there from the Greeks or possibly the Celts at the dawn of modern time. Greyhounds were admired for their grace and elegance and also as canine warriors, marching alongside their masters into battle.

While the Greyhound was popular among Roman men, the society ladies of the era found the breed too large to interact with, and, through their desire for a more petite but just as elegant and stylish hound, they eventually developed the Italian Greyhound, quite literally one of a myriad of lapdogs bred at the time.

The Romans were the first people to treat their dogs in a way we would recognise as being similar to how dogs are treated in the modern western world. They were welcomed into the home and pampered like children. Instead of relying on food scraps tossed from the table or whatever they could garner themselves from hunting, Greyhounds in Roman times were fed a regular structured diet.

The Greyhound also figured just as prominently in Roman mythology as it did in Greek. One of the best-known stories is that of the Greyhound Lelaps, the one-time property of Diana, the goddess of the hunt. Legend has it that Lelaps was involved in the protracted course of a hare when both he and his quarry

The Forest Laws, which were in force in he Middle Ages, meant the Greyhound was exclusively owned by the nobility.

many thousands of Greyhounds that had been travelling with Roman armies being abandoned throughout Europe. But for the help of some Irish priests, who looked after Greyhounds and perpetuated the breed during the aftermath of the fall of the Roman Empire, it could well have become extinct. Many of the clergy enjoyed increased prosperity through breeding Greyhounds for the aristocracy, who became so enchanted with the Greyhound that they wanted them all for themselves. Gradually, over a period of time, the Greyhound became the preserve of the elite members of society.

Throughout the Dark Ages, the Greyhound was used for hunting by the nobility and for that to continue on an exclusive basis the 'Forest Laws' were enacted in the Middle Ages. The laws prohibited commoners from hunting on land owned by nobles without permission – in some cases, transgressors faced execution.

There is a school of thought that we can actually thank the Forest Laws for the emergence of the colours brindle and red that make the Greyhound such a pleasing creature to look at. The theory goes that in order to defy the ban on owning Greyhounds, commoners bred those colours into the dog in order to make them less visible in wooded areas. That, however, flies in the face of the view that Lord Orford was responsible for introducing the colour brindle in the 18th century.

were turned to stone by the gods, who took the action to prevent the death of the hare. The scene can be found on numerous artefacts from the era.

STRUGGLE FOR SURVIVAL

The fall of the west of the Roman Empire in AD476 and the continuing battle for the eastern part of the domain resulted in

A GREAT ENGLISH ECCENTRIC

Lord Orford was an 18th century eccentric nobleman whose enthusiasm for Greyhound racing ultimately turned into an obsession that killed him. He was responsible for the first public coursing club at Swaffham in Norfolk in 1776 and it was perhaps with his coursing interests in mind that he is believed to have come up with an idea that most of his contemporaries thought barmy – and others believed to be far worse.

At his time, Greyhounds fell into two categories: those with a smooth coat and those with a rough coat. The smooth-coated were generally considered smaller and faster than their rough-coated counterparts. Lord Orford believed that by mating a female Bulldog and a Greyhound, he could create a dog with courage and determination. Also, with the influence of the smooth-haired Bulldog, he could produce a soft, smooth-haired animal.

Many attribute the Greyhound's smooth coat to the work of Lord Orford and so, too, the brindle colour, although earlier paintings would seem to contradict this and perhaps back the theory that the Forest Laws were in some way influential. Perhaps it is more accurate to say that any coupling with a Bulldog would have strengthened the brindle strain.

Lord Orford was also famous as the owner of Czarina, one of the most well-known coursing Greyhounds of all time, who won 47 matches in succession. Orford's determination to see her course, after escaping from a secure unit where he had been detained as a result of his alleged mental instability, ended in tragedy. He fell from his horse while celebrating yet another win for Czarina and suffered injuries that proved fatal.

Czarina and Maria in the match that ended in the death of Lord Orford.

The Greyhound was welcomed with great enthusiasm in America.

THE ELITE GREYHOUND

Germany was the first country to implement Forest Laws in the 6th century, but the English took it a step further in 1014 when King Canute introduced laws that meant only the aristocracy were allowed to own Greyhounds. So began a dark period as Canute ordered that dogs thought capable of competing against Greyhounds, in terms of speed and agility, be handicapped – in some cases, by having their hind leg tendon cut.

The status of the Greyhound within society during this period was as high as it had ever been in Ancient Egypt, so much so that anyone found guilty of killing a Greyhound faced the possibility of being executed.

It was not only the English nobility that coveted the Greyhound. The breed was popular all over Europe for its hunting qualities, in particular in France. In fact, a number of the French aristocracy, including Charles V and Henry II, include a Greyhound (or several) on their coat of arms.

In the mid to late 1500s, James I was a big fan of hare coursing and used to have his own team of Greyhounds to course on the vast open plains at Newmarket in Suffolk. It was also around this time that the power of the Forest Laws began to diminish and commoners were allowed to own Greyhounds.

The breed's popularity continued during the Tudor period – between the late 1400s and 1600 – and Henry VII and his son, Henry VIII, were known to be big fans of the breed. Clearly that was something the latter passed on to his daughter, Elizabeth I, who was influential in the shaping of modern-day coursing, as we will see later.

THE GREYHOUND IN AMERICA

Greyhounds had arrived in numbers in America in the mid-1800s with the flood of immigrants from England and

THE ARTIFICIAL LURE

The popularity of hare coursing in the UK in the late-1800s begat an experiment to simulate the practice behind an artificial lure at Welsh Harp, a district of Hendon, north London, in 1876. Utilising a dummy hare on a sledge, which was pulled by a hand-cranked winder, the organisers staged the contest over a straight grass course of 400 yards. It was won by a Greyhound called Charming Nell, who goes on record as having won the first Greyhound race behind a mechanical lure anywhere in the world.

The concept, however, did not catch on and lovers of Greyhound sport continued to indulge their passion for coursing, but the idea of mechanical hare racing was not abandoned, just put on the back burner.

That was until 1912 when an American by the name of Patrick Owen Smith invented a mechanical lure that could travel around an oval circuit, unlike the crude experiment at Hendon almost 40 years earlier that was confined to a straight course. The first oval Greyhound track was developed at Emeryville in California in 1919. But it was not all plain sailing. Greyhound racing took some time to become popular in America and it was not until the introduction of floodlights, which allowed racing to take place in the evenings, that the crowds began flocking to the tracks and more venues started to open.

Ireland. And one person who quickly became a fan was Lt. Colonel George Custer. He was rarely without a Greyhound around him. In fact, his team of Greyhounds often numbered 14 and more.

Greyhounds were popular with US cavalry officers serving in the West in the mid-1800s primarily for their ability to bring down game, which later became food for the cavalrymen. They were also valued for their fabulous eyesight with which they were able to spot movement – and potential danger – in the distance. They were, in effect, used as scouts.

It is now part of legend that the night before the Battle of the Little Bighorn, in which Custer and the Seventh Cavalry were wiped out by the Sioux and Cheyenne Indians, the Lt. General staged Jackrabbit coursing on the plains of Montana. Custer's Greyhounds were a little more fortunate than their master. On his orders, they were sent out of the area after the coursing and were accompanied by their regular handler, James H. Kelly, to safety, avoiding certain death should they have remained in the area as the battle ensued.

GREYHOUND RACING COMES TO BRITAIN

The new sport across the Atlantic was soon in the news in the UK. But, ironically, it was an American, Charles Munn, along with partners Brigadier General A.C. Critchley and Sir William Gentle, who latched on to how lucrative Greyhound racing could be. The three of them pooled their resources and formed a company, the Greyhound Racing Association, and the first promoter of the sport in Britain was born.

The decision was taken to build the first track in Manchester. GRA reasoned that developing a venue in what is the largest city in Lancashire made sense, as the county was a hotbed of coursing. It also made logistical sense, as a good supply of dogs from the coursing fraternity was close at hand.

The enthusiasm for racing by the GRA was not mirrored by that of coursing owners and trainers whose apathy resulted in their virtual non-participation in the first meeting at Belle Vue on 24 July 1926, which was made up of dogs brought in by the GRA from further afield. A crowd of 1,700 witnessed the first meeting of six races, the first of which, over 440 yards, was won by a Greyhound called Mistley. Two meetings later, the crowd had risen to 16,000 and the sport was on its way.

Coursing continued to be popular, but because it took place in rural locations, meetings were difficult for followers that lived in towns and cities to attend.

Conversely, Greyhound tracks could be built in urban areas because stadiums took up only a fraction of the space required by coursing.

Not only did track racing make Greyhound sport accessible to those that were already fans, it also introduced a whole new group of people who had previously not had the time or the wherewithal to get to coursing meetings.

More tracks followed and, in June 1927, a deal was struck to stage Greyhound racing at White City. The west London venue had been built for the 1908 Olympics, but it proved the perfect venue for Greyhound racing and soon became the sport's flagship and home of the Greyhound Derby.

In December 1927, 28 racecourse promoters met at Wembley Stadium to consider the establishment of a Greyhound Club, similar to horse racing's Jockey Club. The National Greyhound Racing Club was formed in January 1928 and the first Rules of Racing was published the following April.

THE GOLDEN AGE

The popularity of Greyhound racing continued to rise through the 1930s. Some extremely charismatic performers helped. In particular, Mick The Miller, twice the winner of the Derby, whose celebrity was up there with the biggest stars of the day. He even starred in a film, *Wild Boy*, in 1935.

Greyhound racing attracted

A CHANGE TO THE BETTING LAWS

In those days you went to the track if you wanted a bet. But in May 1960 the Labour government of the day introduced the Betting and Gambling Act, which, from September 1961, meant punters could place their wagers off-course on the high street in the newly legalised betting shops. The convenience of being able to use betting shops meant punters did not need to attend the tracks, and it was not long before that began to impact on attendances.

The popularity of bookmakers has in the ensuing years gone through the roof and one-time street-corner bookies, such as Corals, Ladbrokes and William Hill have become multi-national corporations and household names. They have also bought Greyhound tracks and their venues form the backbone of BAGS (Bookmakers Afternoon Greyhound Service), which was created by the bookmakers in 1967 to provide a betting event in the shops between horse races.

attendances second only to those at football matches in the years that followed the Second World War. Derby finals at White City in 1940s and1950s enjoyed attendances in excess of 60,000 – and the sport even had its own daily newspaper, the *Greyhound Express*.

There were more than 150 tracks racing under the NGRC Rules of Racing and those of the independent – 'flapping' – sector in the UK when the sport was at its height as Greyhound racing enjoyed continued success in the 1960s, but difficult times were only around the corner.

MODERN TIMES

The following years have seen the closure of more than 70 per cent of tracks operating under the

NGRC code and almost all the independents as tracks as the ever-increasing power of the betting shops, and much greater competition for the leisure pound, has seen customers leave the sport in droves.

On 16 August 2008 the Greyhound industry in the UK was dealt a major blow with the closure of Walthamstow Stadium in east London to make way for affordable housing. The track was the flagship venue since it opened in 1933 and its demise meant that Wimbledon reamained as the only Greyhound track in the UK with a London postcode – there were 33 in the capital when the sport was at its height.

At the beginning of 2009 the NGRC and BGRB (British

Greyhound Racing Board) were morphed into the Greyhound Board of Great Britain at the behest of the Government-commissioned Report into Greyhound Racing, carried out by Lord Donoughue of Aston.

There are now just 27 race tracks in the UK, and as the value of land for residential and commercial purposes rises, it seems inevitable that more will close.

THE RISE AND FALL OF COURSING

Hare coursing in the UK became a thing of the past in February 2005 when the Hunting Bill 2004 was enacted, which made it illegal to hunt with dogs. It meant that a sport that stretched back as far as time itself ceased to be at the

The coursing fraternity turned their backs on track racing.

Coursing Greyhounds, North Wales c.1875.

earned by a Greyhound's ability to work the hare.

The points system is: 1-3 points for speed, 2-3 points for the go-by, 1 point for the turn, 1/2 point for the wrench, 1-2 points for the kill, and 1 point for the trip. Points are awarded by a judge who supervises the course from horse back.

The Swaffham Coursing Club based in Norfolk in the UK was the first public coursing club when created in 1776 by Lord Orford. The east of England (Cambridgeshire, Norfolk and Suffolk, in particular) was popular for coursing primarily because it is a fertile breeding ground for hares. Popularity of the sport grew as increased prosperity enabled the increase in Greyhound ownership and the ability through an improved railway system to travel into the countryside to watch events take place. Consequently, more clubs were formed, and in 1837 the first Waterloo Cup was held on the Altcar estate owned by Lord Sefton near Liverpool, north-west Lancashire.

It soon became an event to see and to be seen at, as those from the privileged classes made their way up from London and Greyhound sport enthusiasts from throughout the country converged on Merseyside in numbers on some occasions just shy of 100,000. Like any event, the Waterloo Cup needed a signature performer and along came Master McGrath to fill that role. The dog, bred in County Waterford in Ireland and owned by Lord

stroke of the ministerial pen.

Greyhounds have been coursed behind live game as far back as ancient Egypt but the practice did not have its own set of rules until 1561. That is when, at the behest of Queen Elizabeth I, Thomas Mowbray, the Duke of Norfolk, created for coursing a set of rules that would become known as the Law of the Leash.

Queen Elizabeth I took the view that Greyhounds were at an unfair advantage over the hare and the quarry would enjoy more of a level playing field if it was given a head start over its adversary. The new rules dictated that the hound's quarry would be given a start of between 50 to 100 yards before the Greyhounds were slipped, in pairs, and the course would commence. Over the years, the rules governing coursing have evolved, and, in latter years, the winner was decided on points

The Waterloo Cup has always been the premier event of the coursing calendar.
Photo: Steve Nash.

Lurgan, won the event an unprecedented three times, in 1868, 1869 and 1871, and further raised its profile. Master McGrath is so famous that the celebrated Irish musical groups *The Clancy Brothers* and *The Dubliners* had a hit with a song named in his honour and recalling his first Altcar victory in 1869. Also, his owner, Lord Lurgan, was requested to meet with Queen Victoria, who was herself a big fan of Master McGrath.

As fantastic as the achievement of Master McGrath was, it did not take long before it was surpassed. The name of Fullerton was the next to touch the lips of everybody and anybody that professed to have even a passing interest in 'the field' – as coursing became known in later years. Fullerton secured the Waterloo Cup a record four times.

The popularity of coursing was ensured for many years by the likes of Master McGrath and Fullerton, but with the advent of track racing in 1926, those from urban areas that had hitherto travelled into the countryside for their Greyhound action could now get it closer to home. Interest in coursing began to wane in the shadow of a burgeoning passion for track racing. The sport continued to be popular among country people and the Waterloo Cup maintained a high profile in the sport's calendar.

But because it involved the use of live hares – a small minority of whom would be killed by the Greyhounds – coursing became controversial and ultimately attracted the attention of the anti-blood sports lobby that staged protests at the major fixtures. The Labour party was voted into power in 1997 with a manifesto that included a pledge to ban hunting with hounds, which was primarily targeted at the hunt but embraced coursing as well, and when the Hunting Bill successfully made its way through House of Commons and the Lords, they achieved their objective.

The Irish Greyhound authorities compromised to pressure for the anti-blood sports bodies when muzzling coursing Greyhounds many years ago – something their British counterparts refused to do – and that is perhaps why park coursing continues to do relatively well in Ireland.

ADOPTING A GREYHOUND

Chapter 4

W hy a Greyhound? There is such a huge choice of breeds available to the prospective owner, so what is it about the Greyhound that stands out and says "take me home"? It's a difficult question to answer, as there is something unique and appealing about every breed, and it is as much a case of beauty being in the eye of the beholder as any thing else.

Before you decide to take on a Greyhound, or any other breed for that matter, you must consider whether you can look after it properly. If you work, can you arrange for the dog to be let out of the house often enough during the day? Do you have enough space in your home for the dog to live comfortably? Are there any other problems likely to be created by having a pet in your home?

A SUITABLE HOME

We all have our idea of the perfect environment for the Greyhound to live in. Having lived in a semi-rural location for much of my life, I have been brought up to believe that dogs should have access to a decent-sized garden or yard and the living accommodation should be large and roomy.

Not everybody with an interest in providing a home for a retired Greyhound can offer such a set-up, but that does not mean they cannot make excellent adopters. What is important is that the new owner cares enough about the Greyhound to take on the responsibility to make up for any shortcomings that may exist in accommodation. The absence of a garden or yard which would allow the dog the chance to relieve himself at his or her will, can be overcome just as long as the adopter makes adequate arrangements for the dog to be

taken out at regular intervals, preferably at the same time every day. The dog should be taken out a minimum of four times a day, and more often in the beginning. Once the dog develops a routine, he or she will become used to being out at certain times of the day and night and his toileting habits will be adjusted accordingly.

While on the subject of accommodation, it is appropriate to consider the implications on your dog of moving house should the situation present itself. It is said moving is one of the most stressful things a person can do. With so many things to think of, it is easy to overlook your dog and, in the confusion, your dog can be lost of injured.

Before moving, it might be prudent to take a picture of your dog just in case he goes missing during the move. Keep your dog confined to one room while the

The Greyhound adapts remarkably well to a life of leisure.

move is in progress, and complete a thorough check on your new premises on arrival just to make sure there are no security issues before you allow the animal into the new home. Once you have settled in, do not forget to change your personal details with the holder of your dog's microchip details and also his dog tag or collar identification.If your dog travels with you, always tape your temporary phone number on his tag.

FAMILY SET-UP

In my experience, Greyhounds are the most adaptable of pets. They will only do as much or as little as you require of them, which means they are suitable for people of all ages. Greyhounds are probably not as active as most other breeds. Given that they

spend most of their younger life racing around the tracks or up the coursing field, they are content to spend their latter years enjoying their leisure. But they can be smashing fun doing all the things you would expect of the domestic animal – playing fetch, chasing around with other dogs, and taking part in most other activities that you would expect them to.

Most Greyhounds are extremely good walkers on the lead. That comes from years of experience when being exercised as a member of a pack at the Greyhound training centre. They are affectionate, loyal and considerate.

LIVING WITH CHILDREN

Greyhound generally mix well with children, but it is prudent to observe a few golden rules.

Most importantly, never introduce a Greyhound to a child without first making use of a muzzle. The dog should be muzzled (the plastic box type) until you are absolutely sure it is safe for the muzzle to be removed – but always have it at hand in case of emergencies.

Your dog should always have somewhere in the house to go so that he can escape young children, who sometimes cannot help themselves when it comes to poking or prodding dogs and invading their personal space.

Make sure children are given a thorough drilling in what is permissible and what is forbidden when it comes to mixing with your Greyhound. Stress the importance of not disturbing the dog when he is asleep or eating. Call the dog to you instead of

If you supervise initial interactions, the gentle Greyhound is a great companion for children.

going to him, to ensure that he is fully alert.

LIVING WITH DOGS OF AVERAGE SIZE

Molly, our current retired Greyhound, is 10 years old and she was recently introduced to the family's latest member, Bobby, a five-month-old Border Terrier puppy, and she absolutely loves him. Anybody that says the Greyhound cannot get on with other breeds ought to see these two. They play together, eat together and walk together – in fact, they are pretty much inseparable. The Border Terrier even curls into the Greyhound to rest.

Over the years our Greyhounds have cohabitated with other smaller breeds successfully, although I would be a little cautious about mixing Greyhound with the tiny, Toy breeds. Use a muzzle when introducing new canine friends.

LIVING WITH OTHER ANIMALS

The Greyhound is bred to chase – and even though he is in pursuit of an artificial lure when he is on a race track, in his own mind, he is chasing prey. How can he, therefore, be trusted to live with dogs, cats, and other small animals that are kept as pets?

In fact, the Greyhound is remarkably good at 'forgetting' his racing past, and learning to live in harmony with other animals. The key is to bear in mind that every Greyhound is an individual, and not every Greyhound shares the same desire to chase.

The instinct to chase is not confined to the Greyhound. All dogs will chase – it is the instinctive behaviour of canines that hunt for food. A Greyhound pup has no stronger a chase instinct than a Yorkshire Terrier. But the difference is that the Greyhound's instinct is nurtured and encouraged during his training, and it therefore becomes an ingrained behaviour.

However, not all Greyhounds want to chase; some show no interest, and some do so only half-heartedly. These Greyhounds are classed as non-chasers and will never make it as far as the racetrack. When it comes to rehoming, you can be confident that this type of dog will be safe with small dogs and cats.

There is a second category of

CHASING INSTINCT

A Greyhound's instinctive behaviour is to chase.

Some Greyhounds will literally chase anything that moves.

If your Greyhound has a very low prey drive, he will live peacefully with small animals.

Greyhounds who do well at the beginning of their racing careers, but then lose their desire to chase or start interfering with other dogs on the track because they are not really interested in the chase. These dogs are usually retired by the time they are two years old. With careful supervision, this type of Greyhound will learn to live with cats and small dogs. Once again, use of a muzzle keeps your other pets safe during this period.

The third category includes Greyhounds that have done well on the track and raced until the end of their careers. By this time, they are around five years old. Obviously these Greyhounds have a strong chase instinct, which has been rewarded throughout their careers. It is much harder for a Greyhound of this type to 'forget' chasing behaviour, once he has retired from the track.

However, all three types of Greyhound can be retrained to modify their behaviour. The first two types are easier to retrain than the third type because their instinct is not so intense. The third type may be retrainable – but not to the same level as the first two categories. It is important to bear in mind that if a dog can be trained to chase in the first place, he can be retrained to inhibit this behaviour – but it takes time, patience and knowledge. Not every Greyhound will accept small dogs and cats. The adoption agency can hopefully guide you in choosing the correct Greyhound for your home sitiation.

For more information on the chasing instinct, see Chapter Seven: Training and Behaviour.

COMMON MISCONCEPTIONS

Has there ever been a breed more misunderstood by the general public than the Greyhound? I ask the question because so many people still come to me with the same enquiries: Are they aggressive? Should they wear a muzzle all the time? Do they need lots of exercise? Greyhounds always look too skinny.

I still recall the days when, as a trainer, I would be walking a group of four dogs and people would literally dive out of my way for fear of being attacked by my Greyhounds, such was their ignorance. The situation has improved as more and more Greyhounds are being found homes by the burgeoning number of home-finding organisations that are emerging in the UK year on year, but there are still a large number to whom the Greyhound is a closed book. In the United States, over 15,000 Greyhounds are adopted annually

The Greyhound is the subject of a number of misconceptions which gives the wrong impression of the breed.

and the number continues to rise, with more than 300 adoption programmes across the nation.

So, to answer the above:

- Greyhounds are far from aggressive. In fact, you would struggle to find a dog with a gentler nature.
- Prevention is better than cure and I feel it is best for all breeds to wear a muzzle when encountering another breed for the first time. And just like other breeds, it is perfectly safe to remove the muzzle once there is no evidence that the parties involved are going to disagree. It is, however, prudent to use a lightweight muzzle (preferably a plastic-coated racing muzzle) when allowing your Greyhound off a lead. Greyhounds are sighthounds. They may follow a bird, rabbit or another dog. In the US, most Greyhound

programmes stress not letting your Greyhound run freely in an unfenced area because you can never be sure if he will take off. Remember, a Greyhound can be out of sight in just a few seconds and is, therefore, out of your control. Every person that reports the tragic circumstances of their dog being hit by a car will always say, "Well he never did that before". It only takes one time.

If you think your Greyhound will respond to you off-lead, practise in a contained area and never allow free-running exercise if there are any risks involved.

- Greyhounds do not require lots of exercise. They enjoy as much as you are capable of giving them, although a minimum of three walks a day, for around 20 minutes to a half an hour, should always be provided.

- Greyhounds carry virtually no body fat. They may look lean compared to other breeds, but as long as there is enough of a covering to ensure that the ribcage and spine are not visible, the dog is in perfect shape.

GREYHOUND REHOMING ORGANISATIONS

The best place to ensure you get the right dog to suit your lifestyle is your local adoption organisation. In the UK, the Retired Greyhound Trust (RGT) has a network of more than 70 affiliated bodies or branches and there are many, many similar organisations that are independent of the RGT that are only too willing to assist you in your search.

In 1972, the Retired Greyhound Trust was established by the National Greyhound Racing Club and Animal Welfare Trust to address the problem of

Organisations such as the Retired Greyhound Trust work tirelessly to find homes for ex-racers.

In the US, there are many major organisations devoted to rehoming ex racing Greyhounds, such as the National Greyhound Adoption Program (NGAP).

finding suitable homes for Greyhounds once their racing days were over. There is no doubt that the RGT does a tremendous job and it finds homes for somewhere in the region of 4,500 dogs per year, but there are an estimated 9,000 dogs that leave the racing scene every 12 months. The job is immense. Funding comes from a variety of sources. In the case of those bodies that are associated with the Retired Greyhound Trust, a portion of support comes from the Greyhound Board of Great Britain, which, through the Greyhound Fund, distributes monies realised by a voluntary contribution from bookmakers.

Over the years, independent Greyhound rescue centres in UK have been set up by people sympathetic to the needs of the former racing Greyhound. These organisations receive limited funding from an official body – the Retired Greyhound Trust makes available small grants towards home-finding projects – and they operate solely on fundraising activities and donations. Most have their own kennels and conduct their business much the same way as those associated with the Retired Greyhound Trust.

Not all Greyhound groups are the same, and you do not have to pick the first one you go to.

Arrange to visit the rehoming kennels a few times before making a choice.

Check them out the same way you would if you were buying a house. By going to a few, you will be able to tell the difference between them and can then select the group that feels right for you.

In America there are a number of organisations devoted to rehoming ex-racers, with the National Greyhound Adoption Program (NGAP) being one of the most well-known. NGAP was founded in 1989 and has been rehoming Greyhounds ever since. It is highly respected for its state-of-the-art veterinary clinic, which opened in 1995 to fulfill the need for specialised greyhound care. The clinic and

surgical facility performs over 2,000 greyhound procedures under anesthesia annually – more than any other facility in the United States!

FINDING A GREYHOUND

Once you have made contact with a rehoming kennel and explained your interest, you are on the way to adopting a Greyhound. The first move will most probably be an invitation to visit the kennels to meet the Greyhounds that are available for rehoming. The kennels will usually be associated with a track and will handle only the runners that have left the racing system at that particular venue, or it will be independent of any racecourse and endeavour to find homes for Greyhounds regardless of their past.

On visiting a rehoming kennel, you will instantly become aware of the marvellous work they do to prepare the dog for a life outside the racing world. In addition, everything is done to assist the potential adopter to find the right dog to suit their lifestyle. When Greyhounds arrive at the kennels, they are tested for their suitability to live with other animals, their compatibility with children, the age-group to which the dog will most probably be best suited, and, among other things, whether or not they are likely to take time to become house-trained. They will also be 'cat tested' which is where the dogs are checked on their compatibility with the local

GREYHOUND

SCENES FROM THE NATIONAL GREYHOUND ADOPTION PROGRAM HQ.

NGAP is a leading rehoming charity in America and specialises in high-standard veterinary treatment for ex-racers. The facility has recently built a new state-of-the-art kennel complex to house even more Greyhounds.

Kennels allow an impressive amount of room for each dog.

Thre is an indoor run available for resident dogs...

...As well as an outdoor turnout area.

moggie. Using the same method a Greyhound can also be tested for its co-habitability with small dogs. All of that information is then posted on the kennel door of the Greyhound it relates to, which allows the adopter to narrow down his or her search very quickly.

Human nature being what it is, some dogs will be more attractive to the potential adopter and will consequently attract home-providers more quickly than others. Puppies are speedily snapped up, as are certain colours. Blue is

The Greyhound you choose will be reserved while the home check is carried out.

particularly popular and a Greyhound of that shade is not available for very long.

In terms of gender, bitches are rehomed quicker than dogs. It is the policy of the Retired Greyhound Trust that all dogs are neutered and all bitches are spayed before they are handed into the care of their new carers.

WHAT AGE WILL MY GREYHOUND BE?

There was a time, not so long ago, when a Greyhound was considered to be at peak racing condition between three and four years of age, and it followed that retirement would take place at around the age of five.

That, however, has changed in recent years, as an increased number of meetings has heightened physical demand and consequently Greyhounds are required to race more frequently in their younger years. This means Greyhounds suffer a burn-out effect sooner and are generally younger when placed up for adoption than they used to be – probably at around four years.

There will, however, be occasions when, because of injury, a Greyhound will retire from the track sooner. A fractured limb – more commonly the hock – is the likely cause of premature retirement.

THE RIGHT CHOICE

I always advocate that you visit your prospective new best friend at least a couple of times before you sign on the dotted line. Bring along any other dogs that you may have at home in order that they can get used to the potential new housemate. Most homing kennels will allow you to take your prospective new Greyhound out for a walk with your family pet to ascertain their compatibility. It might be that it is love at first sight. Conversely, the dogs may despise each other, in which case it may be that you will have to rethink the whole exercise.

You have chosen the dog you would like to take home, so what is the next step?

THE HOME CHECK

No rehoming organisation worthy of the name will allow a dog to leave its care without first carrying out a thorough examination of the property that will be the dog's new home. Most rehoming bodies have an army of volunteers who perform home checks. The checkers will visit you before the dog is officially allowed to leave the kennels, and only when your home has been approved will you be allowed to receive the dog. The home check involves a careful inspection of the property and the checker will also take the opportunity to ensure the adopter knows the full implications of taking on a retired Greyhound.

One home checker in the southern counties said: "The home check is a chance to see the

FOSTERING GREYHOUNDS

role as a foster carer exists for those people that prefer to take a more active part in the rehabilitation of ex-racing Greyhounds on a long-term basis than just taking one home as a pet. Fosterers provide an invaluable service, as they offer a 'halfway house' between a Greyhound's life in a racing or rescue kennel and what is hopefully a permanent place in a domestic home.

As a foster carer, you will be expected to bring the Greyhound into your home until such a time as a permanent placement can be found for it. A foster carer could have as many as four dogs at any one time for anywhere between a couple of days to a couple of months and sometimes more. The foster home proves invaluable at introducing the former racing or coursing Greyhounds to the aspects of everyday life that they may never have encountered before.

As a foster carer, you need to learn not to become too attached to those dogs in your care because the very nature of the job means they will continually move on.

adopter in his or her own living environment. We usually get to meet the whole family and can stress the demands that may be put upon them by their new member.

"Homes security is an important aspect of our work. We make sure the garden – if there is one – is fully secure. All fencing should be set on solid foundations that precludes burrowing and should be at least 5 ft (1.5 metres) in height to discourage jumpers.

"We will make observations about potential dangers. We might advise that a certain type of flooring will present potential slipping problems; that it is impractical to have work and table surfaces at a height at which the dog will be able to steal from

them, and a whole assortment of other issues that may be realised during the check."

Where other pets are already present in the home it is the responsibility of the checker to ascertain the likelihood of the Greyhound being able to integrate successfully. The home checker added: "The general condition and well-being of the other pet will also give us some indication of how well the Greyhound will be cared for."

GETTING READY
You must ensure your home is fully prepared for your dog when you bring him home for the first time. It is important to secure your garden – make sure there are no areas through which your dog can escape. Ensure the house is

safe – are there any areas that might be a problem? It is fair to assume that a family with young children will have made it free from danger – stairs, windows, heights, heat – and you should think along the same lines with your dog.

Also remember, the average Greyhound stands at just about the same height as many worktops and home appliances, such as ovens. Be mindful of this and alive to the dangers they present.

BUYING EQUIPMENT

CRATE
It is handy to have a crate about the home, even if you do not use it frequently. Greyhounds – just as other breeds – are susceptible to bouts of anxiety and at times of

distress a sanctuary offered by a crate can have an amazingly calming influence. It provides a place where the dog feels safe and enclosed. It is the same feeling a dog gets when he lies under the dining room table or curls up in a corner of the kitchen.

BEDDING

A good heavy-duty waterproof mattress should be purchased to place inside the crate. It should be thick to preclude pressure points on the dog's body, which can lead to partial baldness and pain, and deep enough to provide comfort for the time the dog will spend in the crate.

DOG BED

There are numerous dog beds on the market and it would be easy to make a mistake both in price and quality. If you get the chance, inspect the bed before buying. Make sure the walls of the beds are firm and stay upright when put under pressure. My preference is for a waterproof material that can be hosed down. Make sure the bed is big enough to accommodate a large Greyhound lying flat on his side. Most importantly, be careful not to pay over the odds by comparing like for like before committing yourself to a purchase.

FEEDING BOWLS

For a Greyhound, I would strongly recommend an elevated feeding bowl for the following reasons:

- **Comfort:** Just think of what it must be like to stretch down for your food the way we have expected our dogs to in the past. The result can only be unnecessary pressure on the dog's joints and possible damage to the neck, shoulder and back muscles.
- **Digestion:** We all know how uncomfortable it is to be around a dog with a wind problem. By raising your dog's bowl you are helping considerably the digestion of food and consequently reducing the chance of flatulence as well as bloating and constipation.
- **Practical:** How often have you had to clean up after your clumsy hound has knocked over its water or food bowl? A raised feed station lessens the

Your Greyhound will appreciate a comfortable bed, located in an area that is free from draughts.

A fishtale collar is best suited to the Greyhound.

chance of that happening. I use a fixed double feeding stand – one for water, the other for food – using 25-cm stainless-steel bowls. It is prudent to use an adjustable feeding stand for puppies, which can be increased in height as the puppy grows.

If, however, funds are short and you cannot afford to purchase a feeding stand, then an upturned bucket can perform the same function, albeit slightly less securely.

COLLAR AND LEAD

Selecting the correct collar for your Greyhound is more important than you might think. Greyhounds are infamous for their ability to escape from their collars, mainly because they have a neck bigger and wider than their heads, which makes it easy to back out and escape.

The collar most used and considered to be the best for the job is the Martingale. The latter can also be left on the dog and used as a house collar, which gives the handler extra control about the house when your dog can become unruly when the doorbell goes, etc.

For outside wear, I prefer a good, bridle leather, fishtail collar (also known as a safety collar) and lead. The fishtail design widens to approximately 2.5 inches (6.35 cms) at its widest point, which makes escape difficult.

I have a preference for long leads – at the least, 48 inches (122 cms) and ideally slightly longer. I think that comes from the days when it was usual to walk a pack of four dogs at a time. Shorter leads, however, are probably more suitable when walking in built-up areas, when more control over the dog is required.

MUZZLE

It is important to have a muzzle to hand, not because the Greyhound is any more aggressive than any other breed but as a precaution against those times when it may be prudent, such as introducing your dog to other pets and having maintenance work carried out, such as nail-cutting. It is because of the muzzle – mandatory when Greyhounds are involved in organised racing – that the breed is still wrongly viewed by some as being a danger to other animals.

The type of muzzle used for racing in the UK and Ireland is a lightweight wire one, and a plastic-covered version of that is popular among those who take on

A plastic kennel muzzle should be used when you and your Greyhound are out in public places.

retired Greyhounds, as it allows dogs to exercise in comfort and safety both on and off the lead.

The plastic kennel muzzle is also popular. It is heavier and more durable than the wire version and is more practical for everyday use. Most home-finding bodies will have their own shop to supply the essential items and to make a little money for its rehoming activities. You will almost certainly be able to secure the muzzle you require from one of these.

HARNESS
Harnesses are becoming more popular with Greyhound owners in the UK. My biggest bugbear about them is that, in some cases, you almost need a degree in engineering to work out how they are placed on the dog correctly.

Your Greyhound may take some time to get used to a harness because it may well be the first time he has experienced wearing one. The type of harness I prefer is one made from polar fleece. It is soft on the skin and chaffing is reduced to a minimum.

For those dogs that pull – which is rare among Greyhounds – I would recommend the Halti harness. This is specifically designed by Dr Roger Mugford, the well-known UK-based animal psychologist, to be used on those dogs whose reason for being seems to be to stretch the arm of the person at the other end of the lead. The Gentle Leader collar is another popular option, which can be bought online.

DOG BOOTS
There's a whole assortment of foot problems that dogs, including Greyhounds, can suffer from, and a boot is perfect for protecting a delicate area, or even just keeping on a bandage. I prefer the lace-up type where the uppers are made from bonded vinyl and the sole is a non-slip PVC. These are effective and good value for money. I find size three usually fits the average-sized Greyhound.

WALKING-OUT COAT
Greyhounds carry little body fat and are, therefore, more likely than other breeds to feel the cold. It makes sense to have a coat at hand for whenever your dog is feeling the effects of the weather or just suffering from a slight chill.

A double-layered fleece kennel coat is ideal for indoor use, but you will also need a walking-out coat for when your dog is outside. In my opinion, the best type is fleece-lined, which has a waterproof PU outer fabric. You may be able to buy these from your adoption centre.

GROOMING EQUIPMENT
It is important to obtain the best equipment. As far as the Greyhound is concerned, I would recommend the following:

- Fine-toothed Spratts comb – number 73 is probably the most appropriate for Greyhounds
- Rubber grooming mitt
- Body brush
- Horse-hair finishing brush
- Chamois-leather cloth or a tea-towel for putting a final shine on the coat.

TOYS AND GAMES

Perhaps it's my background as a trainer, but I have never thought of Greyhounds and dog toys together in the same sentence. But the breed can and does derive plenty of pleasure from them. There are some marvellous toys on the market, even some that are eco-friendly. Games are my particular favourite, as they test the intelligence of the dog while providing him or her with plenty of entertainment. Dr Roger Mugford offers a number of these through his *Company of Animals* website.

GETTING ID

Once you have your Greyhound, the last thing you want to do is lose him, so you need to make sure he is properly identified. This is, in fact, a legal requirement when your dog is out in public places. Dog tags come in all shapes, sizes and designs, and are almost regarded as a fashion accessory. The tag needs to be engraved with your name and contact details; if your dog has been microchipped, it would be prudent to include that information.

It is worth considering microchipping, as this is a permanent form of ID. A chip, no bigger than a grain of rice, is inserted under the skin in the area of the neck. This contains your contact details and will be scanned if your dog is handed into the police, a dog warden, or rehoming organisation. The home-finding organisation or your vet can make arrangements for your dog to be microchipped. Please be aware that you need to register your details with the microchip provider in order for the information to be linked to the microchip when scanned. Some groups will do this automatically for their adopters; others will leave it to the adopter to do independently.

SETTLING IN

Regardless of the number of precautions you take, something will almost certainly crop up in the first fortnight or so after taking your dog home that you had not bargained for.

It might be that next-door's cat who, in the past, took sitting on your garden wall for granted, gets the shock of its life when you release your new dog into the backyard. Or the window

You will need to get some form of ID for your Greyhound.

cleaners arrive as usual, leave the back gate open, as usual, forgetting or having not been told that the house has a new resident only too keen to explore the outside world.

So make sure you have dotted all the Is and crossed all the Ts before your dog arrives. You need to be aware that your home is a whole new world to your dog and there will be countless new experiences for him to cope with over the first week or so.

If you have other dogs, it is important that the initial introduction is conducted with care and consideration. When I

brought Bobby, our new Border Terrier puppy, home, we supervised initial interactions to make sure relations with Molly, our Greyhound, got off on a good footing.

We brought Bobby into the home in a crate and left him in there while Molly did all the ID checks – sniffing and posturing, as she worked out whether he was friend or foe. We encouraged and rewarded Molly, and only when she relaxed and we were confident that she accepted the newcomer, did we allow Booby out of the crate. In no time, they became the best of friends.

FINDING A VET

As a Greyhound trainer, I always looked for a veterinary surgeon that had experience of racing Greyhounds. Injuries sustained by those competing on the track require understanding and specialised treatment that cannot be given by a general vet.

However, you do not need to be so specific in your search for a suitable vet when taking on a retired Greyhound. Do not always go for the vet whose surgery is closest to your home. Ask fellow dog owners for their opinion.

Probably the most important issue is finding a vet who uses an appropriate anaesthesia protocol and has used it many times on Greyhounds. Greyhounds can easily die under anaesthesia. Barbituates should never be used for a Greyhound. There are several safe protocols but your vet should certainly be aware of the sensitivity that Greyhounds have to anaesthesia since it is quickly absorbed into their bloodstream. Great care must be taken in this area.

It is important that you are always there to reassure your Greyhound as he learns about his new environment. Think of everything that the dog will encounter and try to pre-empt the shock by introducing the dog to the experience – e.g. the washing machine, dishwasher, doorbell, clear glass doors and television – before they are thrust upon him.

Establish a sleeping area for your Greyhound – somewhere secluded and secure – and a drinking and eating area. These can be changed as your dog becomes more familiar with the house and develops favourite areas. While allowing the dog to roam freely around your property, make sure he is wearing a house collar so you retain some control.

For more information on socialising your chapter, see Chapter Seven.

SEPARATION ANXIETY

Your Greyhound has now come into a new home that may or may not have other pets. It originally came from a kennel where it was housed with a large group of other Greyhounds and was surrounded by the smells of all of those other dogs. They ran together, ate together and rested together. If your new Greyhound has not been in a foster home, the transition to a new home may be very stressful and your Greyhound may act out in different ways. A distressed dog may chew the furniture, urinate or defecate in the house, or destroy soft furnishings in an effort to seek you out.

A retired racing Greyhound needs time and patience to settle into his new home.

For advice on dealing with this problem, see Chapter Seven.

HOUSE-TRAINING

If your Greyhound has spent all his life in kennels, he will be used to the routine of being let out into his run to relieve himself, and he will, generally, be in the habit of keeping his bed area clean. He now needs to adapt this routine to a home set-up. Greyhounds are fastidious animals and have no wish to foul their living space, so most will find the transition pretty straightforward.

Start off as if you have a puppy, taking your Greyhound into the garden and showing him his toilet area. When he performs, use a cue word, such as "Busy", so that your Greyhound starts to associate the word with the action. Give him lots of praise before returning to the house. For the first few days, take your Greyhound out at regular intervals so that he understands what is required. In most cases, a Greyhound will have no problem becoming a reliable, house-trained dog.

If you are experiencing problems, go back to basics, and, again, treat your Greyhound as you would a puppy. Give him every opportunity to relieve himself in the correct place, and give him lots of praise and perhaps a treat when he obliges. Remember, a Greyhound wants to be clean, so if he is having accidents in the home, it could be because he is stressed and failing to settle in his new home. However, this is a problem that can be easily solved, so if you are struggling, go back to the rehoming organisation and seek help from a behaviour expert.

PAST LIVES

Most Greyhound adopters find that once the breed has touched their lives, they have an incredible urge to find out everything they can about this fascinating animal. We have brought to you a timeline of how the breed has evolved through the centuries, but what about the life experienced by the dog that you have at the end of your lead – before he or she came to you? How would he have been reared? What were his living conditions like? How was he trained? Did he race on the track or up the field? These are just some of the questions that might have crossed your mind as you get to know, enjoy, and fall in love with your Greyhound.

REARING GREYHOUNDS

The way that racing and coursing Greyhounds are brought up has changed over the years. In the early days, when there was an abundance of land, traffic hardly existed, and life was all together much easier, almost all Greyhounds in Britain and Ireland would have been reared free to roam on the farm. The chief benefits would be the availability of land for galloping, and the ample supply of food such as beef, milk and vegetables. Bread formed the foundation of all meals before the introduction of a complete biscuit. The US has always preferred a more structured and controlled method of rearing which is no less effective.

OPEN REARING

The Irish were particularly good at what was commonly described as 'open rearing'. It was 'open' in as much as the Greyhounds quite literally had complete freedom of the farms – some of which were vast – learning to run and hunt over all types of terrain in a natural environment where there was an abundance of wildlife stimulating the dog's natural instinct to chase. By hunting in packs, consisting mostly of their own siblings, young Greyhounds were honed into future racers the natural way, developing the balance to ride a bump, acquiring the dexterity and nimbleness to sidestep problems when encountering them, and nurturing the acceleration that would prove so valuable when it came to competing on the track or up the field.

Litters would be allowed to roam from around the age of four months right up until their first birthday, and it was often the case that they would not be trained to lead until well into their second year.

Puppies spent most of their time on the land, coming back

63

Open rearing is a system where the strongest and toughest thrive.
Photo: Steve Nash.

home usually only for feeding and to sleep. Accommodation at this early stage of their life was most often a communal barn with a bed of straw.

Feeding would also have been done on a communal basis. There would be a milky feed in the morning and usually a beef or chicken feed in the evening, plus whatever the puppies were able to catch during the day. The 'all-heads-down-together' nature of the feeding can lead to one or two of the weaker members of litters not getting his or her fair share, but any rearer worth his salt would be quick to spot that happening and take necessary measures.

With this type of rearing there is always going to be an element of the survival of the fittest and strongest. Given the nature of things, some youngsters would sustain injury, which, in worst cases, would mean they were unable to fulfil their destiny to

compete on the racetrack. However, advocates of this system reason that to be a cost worth paying for the benefit it brings by injecting a toughness and determination into those that experience it.

A reduction in land available for rearing purposes, allied to the increasing value of top-class racing stock, has resulted in less open rearing in recent years, as many trainers opt for a 'paddock' system (of which you will read later). But one kennel that continues the practice of open rearing – and with excellent results – is that of Michael and Sean Dunphy at Portlaw in County Waterford, Ireland.

The Dunphys are famous for the Droopys prefix and they are among the most successful and best-known breeders and rearers in the world, having won virtually every big race in the racing calendar.

Michael and Sean rear

youngsters on their 150-acre dairy farm. The pups are given a free run of the place and it is not unusual for the brothers to get reports from their neighbours of sightings of their youngsters a couple of miles away, enjoying the freedom of the lush, Irish countryside.

PADDOCK REARING

Paddock rearing is more often practised in the UK, Ireland and US these days and it is arguably as effective as open rearing, considering it is used by leading names such as Nick Savva, Ian Greaves, Pat Dalton and Graham Holland.

Graham Holland is a former England-based trainer who switched his base to County Tipperary in Ireland at the beginning of the millennium. He has had some outstanding results as a trainer and a breeder since he moved across the Irish Sea.

Of the paddock rearing system, Holland said, "It is a safer way to bring up dogs, for a number of reasons, but perhaps most importantly because it gives total control to the person rearing the puppies.

"There are obvious dangers with the open system. Allowing a group of up 20 to 30 dogs – which can be the case in open rearing – to run mad across the countryside means the chances of them getting injured is extremely high. But, with paddock rearing, I can prepare and maintain the ground they exercise on – fill in any holes and eliminate any potential hazards.

"In addition, paddock rearing allows us to put smaller groups together; gives us the option of mixing and matching puppies to create more harmonious rearing and ensure every dog – regardless of temperament – gets a fair chance to reach his or her potential."

Holland disagrees with the theory that the best dogs will always rise to the top in an open rearing system. He added, "He or she might be the best dog but he might also be the unluckiest dog. Luck has a great part to play in all of this, and if you eliminate those dangers that you have control over, you are doing the best for the dog."

As part of the paddock system, puppies will be moved into bigger areas in which to exercise as they grow, starting off at around three to four months in the smallest and being in the largest paddock on the premises by the time they are around 10 months old. Each paddock will also house a shed where the puppies live through their rearing.

Paddock rearing has always been the most popular method of bringing up youngsters in the US and, again, it has stood the test of time. The American preference is for keeping siblings together but separating them into groups of three or four to lessen the chances of conflict, make rearing more manageable and to maximize the use of the land.

In the US, as in the other countries where paddock rearing is employed, puppies as they age graduate to larger paddocks up

It is easier to keep closer check on Greyhounds reared in paddocks.

until the age of 12 months when their schooling will begin.

SCHOOLING

At around 12 months – sometimes later in the case of larger dogs and bitches – Greyhounds in the UK and Ireland will begin the schooling process. This is quite literally what it sounds, as youngsters are introduced to the mechanical lure for the first time and are encouraged to race around the track, starting from a set of traps. Some Greyhounds are naturals and will take to racing very quickly; others will need a bit more coaxing; and there will also be some that refuse point blank to have anything to do with racing and will not chase the artificial lure.

The type of lure used has changed over the years. In most cases in the UK and Ireland, tracks have abandoned the Sumner and McKee lures so

popular in the past and opted for the Swaffham hare, which is easier and, perhaps more pertinently, cheaper to maintain. The Swaffham is not that different to the McKee, as it runs at ground level around the perimeter of the racecourse. However, the McKee lure would be a more realistic dummy hare, whereas the Swaffham bait is an unconvincing windsock that makes little or no noise. The McKee is far more audible as it travels around the track. The significance of that last point is that many dogs chase not only by sight, they are also stimulated by noise, the absence of which in the case of the Swaffham makes chasing it a less than tantalising prospect.

Given the varying degrees to which puppies take to chasing, there is no determinable length of time for schooling, although the average duration for novice to chase with determination, purpose and some track craft is approximately a month. The schooling process begins by releasing the Greyhound by hand, and allowing him to complete just a quarter of the track at a time. By giving the Greyhound a short burst at a time, the schooler is maintaining the Greyhound's interest and eliminating the likelihood of him becoming bored or distracted. Using this method, it does not take long before the youngster is completing a full lap of the track with total enthusiasm.

The Greyhound is then introduced to the starting traps. Firstly, the schooler will just walk the Greyhound through the traps, ensuring the dog knows the correct way in and out. Once this is established, the next step is to place the Greyhound in the boxes and, through a period of trial and error, the puppy will eventually understand what is expected of him.

Once it is considered to be fully engaged with the track – by that I mean, he is fully committed to chasing the lure without any interest in obstructing or interfering other runners – the puppy will be given his qualifying trials. These take place at a proper racecourse, licensed by the authorities, as opposed to schooling, which takes place at tracks dedicated purely to that purpose. It is usual to have three qualifying trials –

A Greyhound must learn to come out of the traps and chase the artificial lure.

two in company and one solo. This helps the racing authorities to establish the ability of the Greyhound, his style of running, and, perhaps most importantly, that he is genuinely chasing the lure and is not a 'fighter'. Greyhounds that are repeatedly aggressive towards others during a race or trial will be barred from the track.

The whirligig, a manually operated arm, plays a pivotal role in the early education process of young racers in the US. From the age of 12 months, possibly even younger, puppies are given the opportunity to prove their desire and develop the ability to chase

the whirligig lure, which is temptingly kept just ahead of their nose.

Some rearers in the US will introduce their charges to the starting traps at a young age. It might be that a set of traps is kept in the field where loading and releasing will be conducted from time to time. All of which should mean that by the time they reach the track for schooling they are familiar with the process of going into the boxes and chasing. Schooling consists of a series of hand slips, increasing the distance with each until such a time as the dog is completing a full circuit of the track.

The inside lure is used in America – and Australia. Trainers are split over whether this is an easier lure to school to than the outside hare, used in the UK and Ireland. My opinion is that a dog is more likely to chase an outside lure given it runs on the ground and looks more realistic. But, as I have said, it is all a matter of opinion.

RACING
The lifestyle experienced by your Greyhound during his time in training would have varied depending on the type of kennel he was placed in by his owner

and the expectations placed upon him. Expectations are built on a couple of factors: the potential the Greyhound had shown in his previous races, if he has had any, and/or the Greyhound's breeding. If your Greyhound was closely related to a particularly successful strain, for instance, the anticipation would be that he would live up to the family reputation.

Conversely, if the Greyhound had shown little on the track and/or was not bred to be anything out of the ordinary, then connections might have had a less optimistic outlook and the Greyhound would be placed accordingly.

In the UK there are two types of Greyhound trainer licensed by the Greyhound Board of Great Britain. There is the Professional Trainer, who is permitted to train an unlimited number of Greyhounds in any ownership, and the Greyhound Trainer, who is allowed to train Greyhounds in any ownership but up to a maximum of 12. As practitioners, trainers are again split into groups: those that are contracted to a track to supply runners exclusively to that venue, those that combine contract and open racing – the latter being more prestigious and highly-competitive – and those that are active only in open racing.

OPEN AND GRADED RACING

The term 'open racing' embraces all the big competitions. All Greyhounds are eligible for these races, but all competitions with the exception of the Derby has a maximum field size, which means only the best are chosen by racing officials at the track hosting the event from entries made by the trainer. Greyhounds that are trained specifically for open competition would, as a general rule, receive a more intensive, specific training regime to those that are trained under the contract system for competition in graded races.

A graded race is an event for six Greyhounds in the UK and Ireland – in Australia most races have eight runners – where the competitors are chosen from the pool of Greyhounds made available by the contract trainers.

The elite Greyhounds compete in open races.   *Photo: Steve Nash.*

A DAY IN THE LIFE OF
A RACING GREYHOUND

A typical day for a dog in a graded kennel would start with being turned out into a paddock while his kennel is cleaned. Most Greyhounds are kennelled in pairs – a dog and bitch is the usual combination, although problematic animals (those with a propensity to aggression) might be kept alone.

After the kennels have been cleaned, the Greyhounds will be exercised. Some will be walked, others galloped. Essential grooming will take place, and the Greyhounds will be let out on to grass paddocks and/or concrete paddocks on a rotation basis for the rest of the day. The one meal of the day will be fed in the early afternoon. Those Greyhounds that are racing that night will be given a light meal and given their main feed of the day when they arrive back from racing in the evening.

An open race kennel would follow a similar pattern, although, given the smaller number of inmates, there would be more time for general care and attention. Greyhounds might be massaged more frequently as well as receiving physiotherapy checks and perhaps even hydrotherapy where appropriate.

A similar pattern would again be followed by the coursing trainer, who, given the banning of the sport in the UK, are nearly all based in Ireland where the sport is still permitted. The coursing season runs between September and March, and during that period a coursing Greyhound would walk between six to eight miles daily and might have 300- to 400-yard gallops, twice or even three times a week. The emphasis is on keeping the Greyhound supremely fit to complete a run through a 32-runner or 64-runner Derby or Oaks Trial Stakes over a cup competition.

The whole of the Irish coursing season is structured around the National Meeting at Clonmel in County Tipperary, traditionally held at the end of January or early February. Regional Trial Stakes for Derby and Oaks take place throughout the season, earning the winners a place in the respective event. The Derby and Oaks are for two-year-old Greyhounds, while older performers have as their Holy Grail the Champion Stakes and Irish Cup, which takes place at Tralee in County Kerry.

Because of their intense racing schedule, the American track Greyhound doesn't do a great deal of work at home. In fact, most of the day involves being turned out into spacious paddocks. Males and females are separated in the paddocks which they occupy in number of 20-30 at a time. The American racing Greyhound is fed once a day.

The person constructing the races in the UK is referred to as 'the grader' and he or she endeavours to bring together six Greyhounds of similar ability to produce a close betting contest and, hopefully, a close and exciting finish. While the Greyhound authorities ensure all dogs receive excellent treatment, those that are considered to be the cream of the crop run in open contests and usually receive more intensive training manifested by a more hands-on approach by the trainer.

Those engaged solely in graded racing would experience top-class care but their training would be based largely around what they do on the track, as, in most

Regular lead walking exercise is combined with free running to allow a Greyhound to build up stamina and fitness.

cases, they race fairly often and maintain their prime condition through racing rather than work done away from the track.

In Ireland the situation is slightly different in respect of how racing is structured. While graded racing forms the backbone of the schedule at the 19 tracks registered with the Irish Greyhound Board (a body that receives funding from the Irish Government), the runners that contest those racers can come from any licensed trainer in the country.

In most cases, Greyhounds in the US are based at kennels on the site of the racetrack. Greyhounds tend to run most of their races at their respective trainer's track in graded competitions, whilst those that are of a higher standard compete in stakes (opens in the UK and Ireland).

FINDING OUT ABOUT YOUR GREYHOUND

Once you have adopted your Greyhound and he has settled into his new home, you will probably want to find out more about his racing and/or coursing career.

While it is likely that microchips will become the sole vehicle for identifying Greyhounds in years to come, in the present day we still rely on ear-markings, which, through a series of letters and numbers, will reveal the identity of the Greyhound. Greyhounds are registered in the UK Stud Book in one ear only, while those from

Ireland and registered with the Irish Coursing Club will have an ear-mark in each ear.

By contacting the respective organisation and giving details of the ear-mark, you will be able to discover the name of your Greyhound. Then, finding out about his racing career should be easy. There are a number of websites that will help you research your Greyhound, including www.igb.ie (the official Irish Greyhound Board), www.thedogs.co.uk (the official Greyhound Board of Great Britain site), for those wishing to know more about American-based racing greyhounds they can contact the National Greyhound Association, Abilene, KS 67410 785-263-466, nga@ngagreyhounds.com.

THE BEST OF CARE

Chapter 6

I t is marvellous when people compliment you on the condition of your dog. There's nothing like it to make your chest swell with pride as your charge dances on the end of his lead, bursting with health and happiness, and showing off a coat that glistens in the sunshine.

That is achievable with some work on your part and the provision of a carefully planned regime of exercise, body maintenance and, most important of all, a nutritionally balanced diet. There is an old saying – "you only get out what you are prepared to put in" – and, believe me, it resonates loud and clear when applied to the care you give to your Greyhound. You owe it to your dog to provide a diet that enables him to live a long and happy life, blessed with good health. However, with the hundreds of food options out

there, how do you make the right choices?

UNDERSTANDING NUTRITION

As a first step, it is helpful to understand the basic components required in a balanced diet so you know what your Greyhound needs.

PROTEIN AND AMINO ACIDS

The proper growth and development of your Greyhound is dependent on him receiving the correct amount of protein, which provides the 'building blocks' in the shape of amino acids that augment the body, bone and muscle of your Greyhound.

Of the 22 amino acids needed to sustain life, a dog can make 12 himself. The other 10 – arginine, histidine, isoleucine, leucine, thionine, phenyalenine, threonine, tryptophan and valine

– are known as essential amino acids and must be obtained over the tongue.

One of the most important roles played by amino acids is to produce the carbon chains required to make glucose for energy. Research has shown that a dog can detect the absence of a single amino acid in his food and will refuse to eat.

Good-quality protein can be found in chicken, eggs and fish.

FATS AND FATTY ACIDS

Dietary fats provide the most concentrated source of energy you can give your dog; essential fatty acids are important to keep your dog's skin and coat healthy, and to maintain the joints and other body systems.

Fats, which can be made in the dog's body from fatty acids in the diet and from metabolites of protein and carbohydrates, also make food more palatable.

A well balanced diet is the key to owning a fit, healthy Greyhound.

Dogs can produce some of the fatty acids they require. Others, however, must arrive through the food chain and these are called essential fatty acids. Fat can be obtained from the fat of animal tissue, while essential fatty acids can be obtained through the supplementation to the diet of the omegas 3, 6 and 9, although it is thought that the use of the latter can dilute the concentration of omega 3 and omega 6.

VITAMINS AND MINERALS

Any high-quality complete food will provide all the vitamins and minerals required to maintain a healthy and happy lifestyle for your dog. Vitamins and minerals work together to provide normal digestion, reproduction, muscle and bone growth, and function.

In addition to using a complete food, vitamins A, D and E can be obtained from liver and eggs. The B vitamins – such as B1 (thiamine), B2 (riboflavin), B3 (niacin), B5 (panothenic acid), B6 (pyridoxine) and B12 (cyanocobalamin) are provided by the likes of liver, eggs, fish and some vegetables.

There are two types of vitamins: those that are fat-soluble and those that are water-soluble. The former, which include vitamins A, D, E and K, are stored in the liver, and the water-soluble type, which includes vitamin C and the Bs, are stored in small quantities in the body and must be replaced daily.

The correct amount of minerals in your dog's body is essential, which is why it is important to use a balanced diet. Like vitamins, minerals they fall into two groups – macro-minerals and micro-minerals. Calcium and phosphorus, magnesium, potassium, sodium and chloride are all macro, while copper, iodine, iron, manganese, selenium and zinc are listed as micro.

CARBOHYDRATES

It is said that as much as half the food you give your Greyhound should be made up of carbohydrates, which, along with protein and fat, is the chief dietary source of energy. Carbohydrates come in two types – soluble and insoluble. The former are most evident in grains such as corn, rice, wheat, barley and oats, while insoluble carbohydrates – also known as fibre – are adequately provided for in all good complete biscuit.

Brown bread is one of the best sources of carbohydrate. Modern-day feeding has meant that the use of bread has almost disappeared from use, but it formed the backbone of the racing and coursing Greyhound's diet in years when many dog-men used it as a chief source of carbohydrate.

My view is that there are better ways of feeding a good complete biscuit, but I would certainly advocate the use of toasted brown bread – perhaps as a breakfast option with a little fish or chicken – as a treat.

WATER

It is impossible to overplay the importance of water. Quite literally, it is necessary for almost every function the dog's body performs. It makes up more than 80 per cent of the body weight of a newborn puppy and 60 per cent of an adult dog; a 10 per cent loss of body water can cause serious problems for your animal.

Water is a great barometer to your dog's health. A sudden stop in drinking may prove an indication that he or she is suffering from ill health, and drinking excessive amounts is also a sign that all is not well. In the case of the latter, it could be that the dog has kidney problems or diabetes.

Fresh water should be available at all times. However, ascertaining exactly what is normal for your individual Greyhound to drink is difficult because all dogs are different and that includes their drinking habits. Your dog's demand for water may increase due to warm weather or after exercise, but over a short period of time you will become accustomed to a regular

pattern and also notice when that pattern changes.

MAKING THE RIGHT CHOICE

It is easy to become completely confused by the claims made by feed companies offering specialised diets for every life stage of your dog, plus organic, vegetarian, and hypoallergenic diets. The truth is, they are all probably very good and effective in their own way. So what sort of food do you choose for your dog?

COMPLETE DRY BISCUIT

Scientifically balanced dry biscuit diets are designed to provide a nutritionally comprehensive feed for your dog through every stage of his life. Complete feeds are perfect for Greyhounds because, as larger dogs, they consume more than a smaller breed and in this regard complete foods are more practical and more cost effective. However, I have always used a complete food as a base

and added meat and vegetables. Additionally, I have always found it pays to spend a little more on the complete biscuit and choose one of the premium brands, which guarantees that only top-quality ingredients are used.

CANNED MEAT AND BISCUIT

The water content in canned meat – at as much at 70 per cent in some cases – puts me off. Canned meat combined with a biscuit was at one time the most common way to feed the domestic dog in this country before the popularisation of the complete dry biscuit. Dogs are generally keen to eat canned meat, but I am not sure that this is the best way to move forward with your feeding regime.

SEMI-MOIST FOOD

This type of food often contains sugar, which means it is hardly an advisable alternative for your dog, given the problems Greyhounds often have with their teeth. Also, it is more likely the

A complete diet is scientifically formulated to cater for your Greyhound's needs.

Canned meat is very appetising but it has a high moisture content.

case that semi-moist food has the least to offer from a nutritional point of view of all the choices available. Many brands also contain artificial favouring and colours.

HOME-COOKED

Feeding this way can be expensive and extremely time-consuming, but it may well appeal to the person with time available who wants to be doubly sure the dog is getting everything he or she requires. To feed this way you should be familiar with canine nutrition to ensure the right amounts of the important ingredients are accounted for within the meal. Product is fresh and the meals are tasty, but this type of feeding is not practical or affordable by everyone.

LIFE-STAGE FEEDING

The age of your Greyhound is one of the initial considerations when deciding on a feeding regime. As he goes through his life and the demands on his body changes, so too do his dietary requirements.

Calculate the cost before opting for a home-cooked diet.

Let us take energy as a typical example. A lively, young puppy or an active, middle-aged dog will use up more energy than an older Greyhound, who is used to leading a more sedentary life. It follows, therefore, that the older dog will require fewer carbohydrates and less fat and protein, which are the three main providers of energy, than its younger counterparts. Another example is that of a bitch during gestation and lactation, who will have her own very specific dietary requirements, and provisions for those will have to be made in her diet.

A lot of it is trial and error. There are some foods that your Greyhound will love and others where he will turn up his nose and refuse to eat. It can be frustrating. But, by spending time considering the options – keeping a watchful eye on how your dog reacts to what is put in front of him and observing how the dog appears physically, particularly in relation to his coat – you will eventually come up with the right balance.

So let us consider the three stages of your Greyhound's development and the feeding regime that should be adopted for each of them. It may well be that you have taken on an adult Greyhound, but it is useful to have an understanding of your dog's metabolism as he develops from puppyhood to maturity.

PUPPY STAGE

For the first two months of a puppy's life, his mother's milk will form the backbone of his nutritional requirements. Through the first milk, the mother passes on antibodies, which the puppy will take on board to fight diseases. It is a natural instinct for a puppy to search for his mother's teat just as soon as he can after birth. There is nothing like a mother's milk for providing all the protection and nutrition a puppy needs at these crucial early stages of life. Puppies that do not follow that pattern should be fed by hand from a bottle, using one of the many excellent powdered milk formulas on the market that are specifically manufactured for newborns.

Puppies will take their food exclusively from their mother for the first 14 to 21 days of life, after which small rations of additional food can be introduced to the diet and fed in tandem with mum's milk. My preference is for cooked minced meat and brown bread soaked in gravy. Milky feeds, such as rice pudding and semolina and/or baby rusks soaked to a pulp in a nutritionally balanced milky formula, are suitable.

By three or four weeks, puppies will be able to get around on their own four feet and supplementary food should be made available to them. This should be placed away from where the puppies rest so they make the effort to reach it. The food should be presented in large, flat trays from which feeding should be done on a communal basis.

After weaning, puppies are usually fed on a communal basis.

Photo: Steve Nash.

Care must be taken to identify those puppies being denied their share of food by their rougher siblings. It might be prudent to feed them individually to ensure they receive enough. Conversely, keep an eye on those that are getting too much, as excessive food can be bad for the digestion and lead to unwanted weight gain. Weaning has now begun, and, as it progresses, the puppy will come to rely less and less on his mother for her milk.

By the time a puppy is seven weeks old, he should be completely weaned from his mother. It might be sooner in some cases – the feeding mother may well need the break, given the stresses and strains put on her by the whole process of giving birth and rearing puppies. With some puppies this process may take longer due to their reluctance to become independent of mum, or perhaps just because they are slower developers.

THE GROWING PUP

Research shows that a growing puppy requires twice as many calories per pound of body weight than an adult dog of the same breed. This is something that should be factored into the feeding regime you have devised to sustain and maintain a healthy, young dog.

Up to three to four months of age, the puppy will have been used to receiving as many as four feeds daily, but that number should be reduced to three before it is cut further to twice daily from the age of nine months approximately. The puppy will

A young Greyhound needs food to supply energy as well as to promote growth.

continue to grow until he is around 14 to 16 months, and during this period the demands on the body and diet will increase as the properly reared youngster will spend little time idle.

Given the opportunity – and a good rearer will facilitate it – a Greyhound puppy will be happy to run all day. He will therefore require a diet that provides the fuel for him to be able to do just that. I always advocate the use of

a nutritionally balanced, complete dry food used in conjunction with raw or cooked meat and cooked fish or tripe to add a little variety. I also like to use vegetables – I am not sure they add a great deal if you are feeding a complete biscuit, but it is something I have always done, and, if nothing else, they provide flavour and fibre.

Where meat makes up 30-40 per cent of the total weight of the meal, it is advisable to use a

complete dry food that contains less protein, perhaps 22-24 per cent. When the dry food content is more than 60 per cent of the diet then a dry food product higher in protein, around 27 per cent, is more suitable. There is also good value in allowing youngsters access to dry food nuts at all times.

The balance of calcium to phosphorus is important whenever a diet is meat heavy (e.g. more than 50 per cent). In such cases it would be sensible to seek the advice of your veterinary surgeon or animal nutritionist to ascertain the correct ratio. Needless to say, these two minerals, and others (such as magnesium, zinc, copper, manganese, iron, iodine and selenium) are important in the development of young canine bodies, and they will be supplied in the correct quantities if you are using a reputable complete dry food.

In my experience, most dogs will drink milk, but it is not good for them. Once a dog is weaned, it seems it loses the enzymes to break down the sugar (lactose) in milk. Consequently, the lactose remains undigested in the gut and can cause stomach upsets and loose stools. Puppies still feeding from mum, however, have the enzyme called lactase, and for a limited period they can drink milk with no harmful effects. Therefore, breakfast, by way of being different for the dog, ought to be made up of a milk formula and a healthy cereal or brown bread. I also like to give an occasional egg to supplement the meal.

Greyhound trainers develop their own, highly specialised feeding methods.

THE FULLY-GROWN GREYHOUND

Greyhound trainers are a cagey lot, and they are loath to give away the secret of the methods they employ to be successful. Some believe the exercise regime they use puts them a length or two ahead of the chasing pack; many more, however, are adamant that the secret is in the feeding they give their dogs. Personally, I feel that those two factors are co-dependent and must be performed to a high level to achieve the best results.

When feeding a racing or coursing Greyhound, you are not only seeking to establish a diet that ticks all the boxes in terms of the requirements of the dog, but also taking into account the additional maintenance requirements caused by such heavy physical demands. That brings into the equation the supplementary use of rehydration fluids. Given the stress that racing and coursing puts on the Greyhound it is sometimes advisable to use antioxidants, an iron supplement, and liver and kidney conditioners.

For the fully-grown Greyhound that is working (e.g. racing, coursing or showing), the basic diet ought to be along the lines of a complete dry food, with a protein content of between 24-27 per cent. Additionally, to keep the food interesting, I advocate the rotation of the following on a daily basis: beef, chicken, fish and tripe. Vegetables should play a part. They are best served cooked and having been through a blender.

FEEDING SENIOR/RETIRED GREYHOUNDS

A properly balanced diet is just as important in the twilight years of a dog's life as it is at the beginning. In fact, it is probably more important because old age will bring with it unique problems which, in the case of a racing or coursing Greyhound, may be compounded by conditions acquired while undertaking those

activities. That is where focus feeding can help your dog live longer and in comfort.

Perhaps we should define what we mean by older dogs. The majority of you will have obtained your Greyhound as an ex-racer. Track dogs can race at five or six years old, but it is more likely they will retire between four and five years when the physical stress of racing begins to take its toll. So, let's add a bit to that and say an older dog is seven years and over.

The first thing to consider is the slow down in activity that your Greyhound will experience in retirement. He or she has been a

worker all his life and suddenly all the activity that is associated with racing – training gallops, long and demanding walks – have been replaced by three leisurely 20-minute walks a day. The chances are, your Greyhound will begin to put on a little weight and it is because of the decreased physical activity and slowed-down metabolism that older dogs need approximately 20 per cent fewer total calories than young dogs.

Obesity is a serious issue, particularly in older dogs, and Greyhounds are no exception. When a dog becomes obese it takes more time for the blood glucose concentrations to return to normal, and a disrupted carbohydrate metabolism can lead to diabetes. This leads on to other complications, which are avoidable with a sensible eating and exercise regime.

These days, it is possible to buy dry food specifically designed for the older dog. It will contain fewer calories but will still have the right levels of protein and fat and is higher in fibre in order to keep the bowel functioning efficiently. Constipation can be a problem with older dogs. Less fat in the diet will mean fewer calories, and a specifically designed senior feed will most probably consist of a fat level of between 10 and 12 per cent. A decreased kidney function can also be an issue when a dog ages, and it is desirable to have less protein in the diet, thus reducing the work the kidneys are required to do.

If you have opted not to feed a complete dry food, it is important

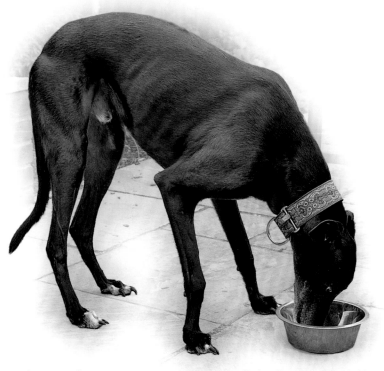

When you rehome an ex-racer, you will need to find a diet that will suit his changed lifestyle.

PROVIDING BONES

We all know how much our dogs love getting stuck into a bone – and the good news is that they are also good for them. Greyhounds are susceptible to bad teeth. Why is not clear, although a number of people I have spoken with about the subject attribute part of the blame to the sloppy type of the food fed by so many of the racing kennels.

A raw bone once a week will reduce the build-up of tartar on your dog's teeth; it will help freshen up his breath, keep him entertained for hours on end, and satisfy any urge to chew the leg of your favourite table or sofa.

While on the subject of teeth, I have found the sticks that are specifically designed by animal food companies to reduce the build-up of tartar – some claim to reduce it by 80 per cent – particularly useful. One a day will help the fight against tooth decay. It is important to stress, however, that brushing is still the most important method of maintaining healthy teeth.

Providing bones and chews will help prevent the build-up of tartar.

WHAT NOT TO FEED

So far we have looked at what to give your dog, but there are also a number of foodstuffs that should never pass over the lips of your most prized possession.

Top of that list is chocolate made for human consumption. Given our universal love of chocolate, it is so easy for your dog to pick some up about the house, so be extra vigilant. Chocolate acts as a stimulant and can cause an increased heart rate or an irregular heartbeat, which could lead on to a heart attack. Chocolate is a diuretic and may also cause diarrhoea and/or the dog to vomit.

Raw onions are also a big no, no, as they can cause a breakdown in your dog's red blood cells, resulting in oxygen deprivation. Salt, grapes (including raising, currants, sultanas etc), raw fish, alcoholic drinks, and caffeinated drinks are among other items to avoid.

It is your duty to inform people likely to come into contact with your dog that the aforementioned are strictly forbidden. Also, be alive to the danger from open tins and glass if your Greyhound gets into household bins. Keep the bin secure. Make sure your Greyhound doesn't scavenge or lift bits of food from outside the home. There may be poison or vermin bait present and the consequences can be a serious illness or even death.

to supplement your dog's feed with a vitamin/mineral supplement, of which there are many on the market. That should ensure there are no deficiencies. Cooked eggs in any form can be enjoyed once a week or so. Cheese, which also acts as an excellent treat for training purposes, can be crumbled on top to give the meal more appeal. Oily fish, such as sardines, are another favourable treat.

Muscle and joint problems, which may have been sustained during the dog's racing career, will probably get markedly worse as old age hits. Arthritis can become a problem. The condition is helped by supplementing your

dog's daily food ration with glucosamine and chondroitin, which should minimise damage to the cartilage in the joints. Glucosamine and chondroitin naturally occur in the bodies of living animals. Younger, healthy dogs make their own to keep their cartilage healthy, but older, infirm dogs that are suffering from joint cartilage problems cannot produce enough, so they require a topping up with powered form.

A teaspoon of sunflower/vegetable/fish oil added to the main meal will help maintain a glossy coat, and some owners swear by a daily tablespoon of cod-liver oil to help creaking joints.

EXERCISE AND MEALTIMES

Just as it is not good for us to spend an hour at the gym and sit down to a big meal immediately afterwards, Greyhounds should not be fed for at the very least one hour before or one hour after feeding.

For obvious reasons it is also sensible not to feed your dog before a long car journey. Just make sure he has a fresh supply of water for the trip.

MAINTAINING THE CORRECT WEIGHT

Establishing the correct weight for your Greyhound is not always easy, but it is important because being overweight or underweight will have a significant bearing on how much your dog enjoys his life – and, more importantly, how long he will live.

IS YOUR GREYHOUND UNDERWEIGHT?

I am sure we have all seen images of underweight animals. They make a pitiful sight. On an underweight Greyhound, his ribs, vertebrae and hip bones will be clearly seen and there will be little or no fat on his bones.

Seriously underfed Greyhounds are more open to bacterial infections and also infestation from parasites. Female Greyhounds will suffer a disruption to their cycle and find that their ability to look after their young will be compromised. Malnourished puppies may suffer from stunted growth, while older, underfed dogs are vulnerable to osteoporosis.

IS YOUR GREYHOUND OVERWEIGHT?

The most obvious signs that your Greyhound is overweight are evidence of fatty deposits over his back, being unable to feel his ribs through a layer of flesh, and a heavy covering of bulk over the hindquarters. Overweight dogs will also appear fleshy around the lower neck region and behave with extreme lethargy.

Research has shown that obesity occurs in 25 per cent of dogs in western societies and that can lead to health risks, such as diabetes and osteoarthritis.

Regular weigh-ins will help you to maintain the correct weight for your Greyhound.

EXERCISING YOUR GREYHOUND

As discussed previously, a Greyhound does not require nearly as much exercise as most people think. If you work on a basic premise of three 20-minute walks per day, your Greyhound will remain in fit, healthy condition.

ROAD WALKING

As the roads have become busier, thus increasing the chance of an accident, road walking Greyhounds has become a less common activity. However, road walking comes with its own benefits and should still be undertaken wherever it is possible, although the first consideration should always be safety. With this in mind, it is sensible to avoid the busy periods. Leave exercise until after 10am and before 5pm. When the weather is warm, avoid walking at the hottest part of the day. Have

As part of a training regime, road walking is used mostly by the trainers of coursing dogs and for of those track Greyhounds that race over an extended distance. Coursing trainers in Ireland are big fans of road walking, sometimes covering up to eight miles in one session to keep their charges fit.

FREE RUNNING

There is nothing as pleasurable as watching your Greyhound enjoying a run. You can almost feel their excitement as they as they gambol around. But before you let your dog off the lead, you must be confident he will return. It is therefore a good idea to practise recalls in a safe and secure environment before going the whole hog and allowing your dog to run free.

To do this, call your Greyhound back to you on a random basis. Give him a big welcome, shower him with praise and, most importantly, reward him with a tasty treat.

When first allowing the dog off-lead, make sure it is done in open countryside – not a small park, but somewhere with a good bit of land where your dog will have space to enjoy himself. Call your dog back frequently, always making a fuss of him and rewarding him with a treat. Coming back to you must be something the dog looks forward to.

Always muzzle your Greyhound when allowing him off-lead, using a plastic-covered racing muzzle.

Road walking will keep your Greyhound's feet in good condition.

your Greyhound wear a muzzle until he is reliable in a social environment.

There are a number of benefits from road walking, including the improved fitness of your dog, keeping your dog fresh and alert by changing the route you walk daily, and feet maintenance, as regular walking on hard roads will keep nail length down and reduce the chance of a sprung toe, which is a dislocation of the toe joint.

VIABLE OPTIONS

If you are unable, or unwilling, to allow your Greyhound off the lead, the next best thing is to use an extending lead. Retractable leads have become very popular but I would not recommend their use with the Greyhound and that is a view shared by the Retired Greyhound Trust. In my opinion the problem is Greyhounds accelerate so quickly that walking on a retractable lead can lead to injuries in the wrong set of circumstances. If you are determined to use a retractable lead then it might be prudent to use them in conjunction with a harness, thus eliminating the potential for a sudden, sharp pull on the neck.

An extra-long lead – perhaps an adaptation of a lead used for the lunging of horses – is more suitable, though particular attention should be paid to not allowing the lead to become tangled around the dog's legs.

SWIMMING

Swimming is an excellent form of exercise that many Greyhounds enjoy. It is fantastic therapy for dogs with muscle and joint injury, as it allows the dog to exercise while eliminating the pressure on the joints that comes when exercising on concrete or grass.

GROOMING

Caring for your Greyhound's coat is not the most difficult job, given its smoothness, but it must be regularly maintained because, just as the most verdant of lawns will become a wild wilderness if left

Your Greyhound will appreciate the opportunity to run at full stretch.

Some Greyhounds enjoy swimming, which provides excellent exercise, particularly if a dog is recovering from injury.

Climatic conditions can affect your Greyhound's coat.

long enough, your hound can have a serious shaggy dog problem if neglected.

The condition of your dog's coat will be influenced by factors other than whether or not it is regularly groomed.

Feeding a nutritionally balanced diet will go a long way to ensuring a healthy skin and will reduce the need for grooming to a minimum. When I was a trainer, my dogs needed very little grooming because of the excellent diet we provided for them.

The climatic conditions your Greyhound lives in will also have an effect on his coat. The colder the climate, the quicker his coat will grow and the more work it will require. So, those

Greyhounds that live outdoors will need more work than those that live in heated quarters.

Mange and other skin conditions may also affect the quality of the coat. *For more information, see Chapter Eight: Health Care.*

Many of you may feel the temptation to employ the services of a professional dog groomer. There are plenty of perfectly qualified people to care for your Greyhound's coat and most will do a first-class job. But I would advocate that you resist that temptation and undertake the job yourself. It is great fun, provides you with bucket-loads of satisfaction, and, perhaps more importantly, creates a smashing

bond between you and your dog.

STEP BY STEP
Call me fussy, but before any grooming is undertaken, I would always make sure the dog is standing correctly – fully square. The forelegs should be upright and the hindquarters outstretched – in the position you would show the dog.

- As the coat is relatively smooth, I start with a fine-toothed Sprats 73 comb. The fine teeth will pick up any evidence of parasites – e.g. fleas and ticks – and also leave the coat smart and orderly.
- Next I use a stiff-bristled body brush (a horse dandy brush

ROUTINE CARE

A stiff bristled brush removes dirt and dust.

You can use guillotine type nail clippers to trim the nails.

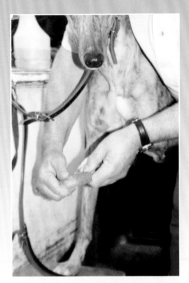

Some people prefer filing the nails to avoid the danger of cutting into the quick.

works well) and with this I vigorously work through the coat to remove dirt and dust. By being fast and firm – be careful not to overdo it – the coat will be left with added vitality.

- The coat is now ready for the horse-hair finishing brush, which helps to bring out a shine.
- I always end the grooming session by running a clean towel or a chamois leather cloth over the back of the dog. It leaves a lovely, gleaming finish.

FEET AND NAIL CARE

You need to make sure your Greyhound's nails are clipped and filed on a regular basis, especially if your dog spends most of his time walking and exercising on grass or a soft surface, such as sand. Road walking will keep nails trim and you may need to clip and file less frequently.

Your veterinary surgeon or a professional groomer will trim your dog's nails. Alternatively, you might prefer to cut them yourself. If you opt for the latter, you must exercise caution so as not to cut the quick – a blood vessel in the nail – because failure to do so will result in it bleeding profusely.

Signs that your Greyhound's nails need to be trimmed are obvious, but if you cannot see

them then that annoying clicking sound of the dog's nails on uncarpeted floors, such as wood, stone or tiles, will definitely give the game away. The consequences of failing to keep your dog's nails to a sensible length are general discomfort for the dog, sore feet and even joint problems.

If you are going to cut the nails yourself, you must decide on the best clippers to use. There are a number of makes on the market, but the Greyhound has large, thick nails so your choice must reflect this.

I have always found the stainless-steel, scissor-style to be the most effective for the larger breeds. Choose a type that has an indentation in the blade to accommodate the nail, as this makes cutting easier. Other makes also have a 'stop cut', which can be preset to govern the amount of nail you dispose of.

STEP BY STEP

* Some handlers prefer to lie the Greyhound down on his side to cut and file the nails. However, I prefer to straddle the dog when I am cutting the nails on the front feet, and then attack those on the hind feet from the respective sides. I believe this gives you more control over the dog.
* Some dogs are particularly awkward about having their nails trimmed. In particularly difficult circumstances, I have found it particularly effective to get a friend to lift the dog off the ground while cutting takes place.
* Be purposeful but careful when cutting, removing just a little at a time. The job is complete when the nail sits above the ground when the foot is flat.
* After cutting, tidy up the nails with a large file, removing split ends.

BATHING

As a Greyhound trainer, I used to bath my dogs regularly in the warmer weather. Bathing not only improved the condition of the coat and deterred parasite infestation, but also seemed to improve their performance on the track, because it made them feel fresher and cleaner. Regular bathing should remain part of your Greyhound's life, particularly in the warmer months.

STEP BY STEP

• First find a suitable place to bathe your dog. When the weather is warmer this may be outdoors, but definitely indoors in the colder months.
• Make sure you provide sensible underfoot conditions – ideally a rubber mat – to eliminate the

PROBLEM SOLVING

If, by cutting into the quick, you should cause the nail to bleed during the trimming process, a styptic pencil will help stem the flow. The bleeding will stop soon enough and it is not a cause for concern.

Crumbling nails is a problem that affects some Greyhounds, and I remember it was a particular problem with one of my old Greyhounds. Supplementing the diet with biotin, zinc gluconate and/or some omega 3 may help. If these fail to correct the problem, if might be prudent to seek veterinary advice.

Always check the general condition of your dog's feet when clipping his nails. Check for signs of chewing, redness and soreness at the bed of the nails, dry and cracked pads and damage to the webbing between the toes. There are a number of possible causes of chewing, which include boredom, itching or even obsessive compulsive disorder (OCD). This is best dealt with by a veterinary surgeon.

Inflammation at the bed of the nail (the point at which the nail joins the toe) may be caused by foreign matter penetrating the skin. Dry and cracked pads are more prevalent in older dogs, There are a number of possible causes, including dietary, exposure to fertilisers or detergents used on floors, or excessive licking.

I regularly use a lubricant that puts moisture back into the pads, but if that is not effective, ask your vet for advice.

EARS AND TEETH

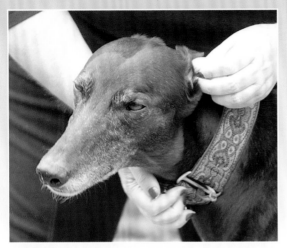

Clean the ears with cotton-wool, making sure you do not probe into the ear canal.

When cleaning your Greyhound's teeth, make sure you use a toothpaste specially formulated for dogs.

chance of your dog slipping.

- Always make sure you have assistance when bathing your Greyhound. As the water gathers in the coat, it weighs heavily on your dog to the point when he will have difficulty standing. Get a friend in to help hold your dog upright while you continue washing.

- Use a shower-head or hose to soak your dog's coat with warm water – not too hot or too cold – and then apply a dog shampoo. Do not use human shampoo, as people have different pH values to dogs - while human skin has a pH of 5.5, your Greyhound has a pH of 7.5. This means that if you use human

shampoo on your pet, it could result in scaling of the skin and general irritation.

- Work the shampoo into the dog's coat and rinse thoroughly. I always recommend you repeat this twice before fully rinsing, making sure all soapy remains are removed from the coat. Shampoo that is left to dry on your dog can cause skin irritation.

- Dry off your dog with a towel. I have never been a fan of blow-drying my dog's hair, although the practice has value when dealing with older dogs in cooler weather when it is important to dry the dog as quickly and efficiently as possible.

CLEANING EARS

Your Greyhound's ears should be cleaned at least once a month. However, if you notice wax at the entry to the ear, it will mean your dog is suffering from a build-up and cleaning should take place more frequently until the problem has been eliminated.

Ears can be cleaned by using a ball of cotton-wool and a small quantity of baby oil. Never use cotton buds, and only clean wax that is visible at the top of the ear. Never poke anything down the ear. Alternatively, you can obtain special drops from your local pet store, which soften wax and also kill any ear mites that may be present in the ear canal.

There are a number of signs that indicate a dog may be

suffering from ear problems. Your dog may shake his head from time to time, he may try to scratch his ear, or you may notice that one or both ears are giving off a nasty odour.

ORAL AND DENTAL HYGIENE

As much as your Greyhound may protest at having his teeth cleaned, he will enjoy the benefits of cleaner teeth and a fresh taste in his mouth. Dental hygiene should be taken seriously with all breeds but Greyhounds, in particular, can experience problems with their teeth.

Make sure you use a toothpaste made specifically for dogs. Paste made for humans includes ingredients that will upset your dog's stomach. For the physical act of brushing, you should use either a pet toothbrush or a rubber finger toothbrush. I prefer

the former, which is made specifically for dogs.

I have always found that straddling the dog – particularly if he is reluctant – is the best way to approach teeth cleaning. Introduce your dog to the taste of the paste by rubbing it into the teeth and gums before you start brushing. Most dog toothpastes are flavoured, which Greyhounds usually find agreeable.

THE OLDER GREYHOUND

Signs that your Greyhound is ageing do not come overnight. They build up over a period of time until it suddenly becomes obvious that the lively character you once knew is no longer as bouncy and vibrant as he used to be.

The first indication of the ageing process may be a little greyness around the muzzle area and the eyes. Your Greyhound

might also begin to lose his shape as his muscle definition – once so sharp and striking – starts to lose the fight against the flab. As a Greyhound ages, his skin may become thinner and he will become vulnerable to injury and bruising. The dog's feet do not escape either, as the pads can harden and crack, while the nails, in some cases, become brittle and crumble. Older dogs are also more susceptible to calluses, sometimes as a result of lying on firm surfaces for long periods of time; a suitable bed will make all the difference here (see page 56).

We have already looked at feeding senior dogs; suffice to say, as the carer of an ageing Greyhound, you must be alive to the problems that afflict dogs as they enter the latter years of their lives. A decrease in activity can lead to an increase in weight, and this is something to be avoided at all costs. Any obvious weight gain will put further strain on your dog's joints, heart and other organs, which will be detrimental to his health and wellbeing. You will probably need to make adjustments to your dog's diet. Research has shown that older dogs require approximately 20 per cent fewer calories than when they were in the full bloom of youth.

The addition of supplements to counter age-related conditions, such as arthritis, is recommended, in particular glucosamine and chondroitin, which help with joints. A daily teaspoon of cod-liver oil can also

The first signs of ageing is usually greying around the muzzle.

prove beneficial; I have also found devil's claw and yucca can make an excellent anti-inflammatory preparation, which is ideal for giving pain-relief to the older dog.

Regular checks-up by your veterinary surgeon are recommended to ensure that your dog enjoys, where possible, a long and healthy old age. Greyhounds are martyrs to their teeth and suffer in particular from gingivitis. This condition is an inflammation of the gums caused by a build-up of plaque.

In addition, subjects of special interest to your vet, include cancer, diabetes, diseases affecting the liver and kidneys, and thyroid problems, all of which are more common in the older Greyhound. Your Greyhound may alsol experience problems with his eyes, such as cataracts, glaucoma, and a condition called dry eye, which is quite literally what it sounds, as the tear duct produces insufficient lubrication for the eye. *For more information on these conditions, see Chapter Eight: Health Care.*

The older members of our canine society are well catered for by veterinary surgeons, many of whom run special forums for their pensioner patients, at which those issues that affect older dogs are discussed. At these sessions your Greyhound can go on to a care programme, which will involve regular tests for age-specific conditions, which include blood tests, urinalysis, X-rays, and heart monitoring.

The older Greyhound will really enjoy his creature comforts.

MAKING ADJUSTMENTS

As your Greyhound ages, you need to keep pace with his physical changes so you can make your home as comfortable as possible.

The older Greyhound will spend more time in his bed, so making sure that his bed is suitable for his needs should be a top priority. There is a whole host of beds on the market, and manufacturers make a myriad of claims, so selecting the right one for your dog can be a difficult assignment. Do not be fooled into buying a flash and colourful bed; make sure you understand the specifics of the mattress before making a decision.

Where older dogs are concerned it is important to secure the right mattress. I favour a visco-elastic material that conforms to the body shape of the animal and offers excellent support. They are considered to be the best for older dogs, in particular those that suffer from joint problems, hip dysplasia, arthritis, or those that are particularly overweight – with all the problems that brings with it.

As reduced mobility will become a factor in later life, it is sensible to place the bed somewhere that is easily accessed by your dog – a location that does not require the Greyhound to climb stairs would be preferable. While on the subject of climbing, it might also be prudent to consider purchasing some steps or a ramp to either

CHANGES IN BEHAVIOUR

As your Greyhound grows older, in common with most other breeds, he may become quite tetchy, so it pays to be cautious, especially when he is asleep. You should take care not to startle a dog when he is asleep, regardless of his age, but you should be extra careful as he gets older.

There is also the possibility that your Greyhound will be prone to accidents in the house. Greyhounds are very proud animals and will be extremely embarrassed if this happens. Accidents such as this occur in older dogs that are suffering from a bladder problem, bowel diseases or colitis. If you suspect a problem, consult your veterinary surgeon.

lean against or rest adjacent to any raised areas in the house. We have discussed the ramp in another chapter when looking at getting into and alighting from a vehicle, but for in-house activity, a small set of three or four steps is probably the best option.

As your Greyhound gets older, his eyesight may deteriorate. This is a difficult time for both you and your dog as you adapt to a changing situation. You will need to get used to taking on more responsibility for the welfare of your dog.

If there is only mild deterioration, your Greyhound may not be able to get around as easily as in the past, but his lifestyle ought not to be too badly compromised. A more acute deterioration will require action. Your dog will still be able to get around, but it might be prudent to take the following precautions:

- Restrict your Greyhound's movement within the house, putting gates at the bottom of your stairs or to prevent access to particular rooms.
- Try not to move furniture, as your Greyhound will learn to find his way about and will become disorientated if the layout changes.
- Find a safe, quiet place for your dog's bed, and keep it there.
- Put a bell on your dog's collar so that you know where he is at all times.
- Restrict access to areas of the garden, such as steps, which could be potentially hazardous.

THE FINAL DECISION

The decision to have your Greyhound euthanased will be the most difficult you make in your dog-owning life. But when the time does arrive, it is important to take into account the interest of your dog more than your own.

Your dog has been diagnosed as being terminally ill. Presumably all avenues of treatment have been explored and it has been decided that nothing can be done to save your dog's life. In this situation, forget about how much hurt you are going to suffer and consider instead that you are doing the best for your dog. He has given you so much devotion, surely your last act of kindness should be to make the decision that is right for your dog.

Of course, you will not reach a decision without talking it over with your veterinary surgeon, who will put you in the picture in respect of the long-term prognosis for your dog. A key factor in making your decision will be the dog's quality of life. If he is able to continue with a normal life – eating and getting around without much pain – then it might be okay to delay a

You need to decide what is best for your old friend.

decision, but, ultimately, take the vet's advice.

Pet hospices are becoming more and more popular. They offer palliative care to your dog prior to nature taking its course, or they give you time to make up your mind about euthanasing your dog. They can be costly, though, and that is an aspect that must be considered. Equally, you should bear in mind that if you delay putting your dog to sleep when there is no hope of him

recovering from an illness, it could prove expensive, especially if you have to buy medication, as is likely to be the case. So, do not feel guilty if you have to make the inevitable decision for financial reasons.

In most cases – especially when dealing with an older Greyhound – you will have some notice of what is about to happen, particularly if the Greyhound is suffering from a terminal illness, such as cancer.

That extra time should be used wisely to prepare for the end.

Handling the loss of a pet is always difficult, but particularly in instances where the animal has become part of family life and there are children involved. Very young children, those up to about 24 months, will not understand what is happening. They will, however, be able to detect that all is not well and when this happens, the parents should offer comfort. In

Does a dog grieve if he loses a close companion?

situations where children are older, it is important not to hide from them what is happening. They will have become attached to their Greyhound.

From personal experience, I can testify that the death of a pet is difficult for the whole family, including other dogs in the home. In the most recent case in my household, we lost two of our three dogs over a three-month period. Kate, a Border Collie-Labrador cross – a rescue that we had obtained from Battersea Dogs Home 12 years earlier – lived to a good age. But following her death, our Greyhound, Rocky, died within three months. To this day, I am convinced this was caused by a broken heart.

This raises the question: do animals grieve? In Rocky's case, I am sure he did. His decline started the day my wife returned from the veterinary surgeon without Kate who, on the advice of the vet, was put to sleep because she was suffering from cancer. Rocky displayed all the signs of grieving. He became listless, disinterested in food, and didn't want to do anything other than lie on his bed all day. His death came when he lost the power of his legs. Numerous tests failed to locate the precise problem, and, considering his case history, the veterinary surgeon that recommended his euthanasia concluded that he most probably died of a broken heart.

As well as experiencing their own pain on the occasion of bereavement, other dogs will sense your sorrow. They will tap into your sadness with empathy.

At this time it is important that you show them nothing has changed. Feed them at the same time and maintain your usual exercise routine. It is important not to indulge your dog if he is grieving. Do not give him treats in an attempt to bring him out of his state of lament. He will come to expect them, and the whole process of moving on with life could be compromised. If anything, he will begin to adopt sorrow as a means to obtaining more treats.

Whether you want to be with your dog when the time for euthanasia arrives is something for you – and only you – to decide. It is not for everybody. If you cannot bring yourself to attend, your veterinary surgeon and his staff will do their best to make your dog feel comfortable. They are professional people who deal with highly charged, emotional situations virtually every day.

The act of euthanasia is performed quickly and efficiently. A concentrated solution of pentobarbital is injected into the animal intravenously. It does not take long – sometimes as few as four or five seconds, possibly longer in a dog with poor circulation – before the dog drifts off to sleep. You may notice the dog's body moving in the moments after he has died. Muscles might contract and legs might move. It can be upsetting, but it will not last for long and soon the body will be at peace.

It will be up to you to decide what you would like to be done with your dog's body. Most of my pets have been buried in my garden at home, but that is something I have regretted because I have moved around so much in the last 20 years or so. The last two dogs that we have lost have been cremated, which, for whatever reason, seems to rest better with me. If you can afford an individual cremation, the ashes can be returned to you in an urn as a keepsake. The alternative is a group cremation, but with that you will not get the dog's individual ashes back.

Pet cemeteries are becoming increasingly popular, so there should be one within driving distance of most people. That is another option.

Closure is important, for you need to move on with your life and be able to enjoy happy memories of time spent with your

In time, you will be able to look back and enjoy the happy memories of time spent with your beloved Greyhound.

Greyhound. It might be that you decide to get another ex-racer after a while and that is the biggest compliment you can pay the dog

that has just passed away. Treasure each and every one of them for their uniqueness and special qualities.

TRAINING &
SOCIALISATION

Chapter 7

When you decided to bring a Greyhound into your life, you probably had dreams of how it was going to be: long walks together, cosy evenings with a Greyhound stretched out on the sofa beside you, and, whenever you returned home, there would always be a special welcome waiting for you.

There is no doubt that you can achieve all this – and much more – with a Greyhound, but like anything that is worth having, you must be prepared to put in the work. A retired Greyhound will need to make major adjustments to fit in with your lifestyle. All he has known is a routine of kennels and racing, and suddenly, he has to learn to live as a pet dog. He has to find a place in your family, and discover what constitutes acceptable behaviour in his new home. He cannot do this on his own – he will need help and guidance from you, right from day one.

We have a great starting point in that the breed has an outstanding temperament. The Greyhound was bred to hunt and he is designed to be the ultimate canine athlete, but, at heart, he is calm, gentle and laid-back. He may be able to reach speeds of 40 miles per hour (64 kmph) on the track, but it does not take him long to discover that your home can give him all the creature comforts he has ever dreamed of.

THE FAMILY PACK
Dogs have been domesticated for some 14,000 years, but luckily for us, they have inherited and retained behaviour from their distant ancestor – the wolf. Greyhounds were developed to hunt alongside man, and never had to live in the wild, but every Greyhound is born with the survival skills and the mentality of a meat-eating predator who hunts in a pack. A wolf living in a pack owes its existence to mutual co-operation and an acceptance of a hierarchy, as this ensures both food and protection. A domesticated dog living among people has exactly the same outlook. He wants food, companionship, and leadership – and it is your job to provide for these needs.

YOUR ROLE
Theories about dog behaviour and methods of training go in and out of fashion, but in reality, nothing has changed from the day when wolves ventured in from the wild to join the family circle. The wolf (and equally the dog) accepts a subservient place in the family pack in return for food and protection. In a dog's

95

Have you got what it takes to be a firm, fair and consistent leader?

eyes, you are his leader and he relies on you to make all the important decisions. This does not mean that you have to act like a dictator or a bully. You are accepted as a leader, without argument, as long as you have the right credentials.

The first part of the job is easy. You are the provider and you are therefore respected because you supply food. In a Greyhound's eyes, you must be the ultimate hunter, because a day never goes by when you cannot find food. The second part of the leader's job description is straightforward, but for some reason we find it hard to achieve. In order for a dog to accept his place in the family pack, he must respect his leader as the decision-maker. A low-ranking pack animal does not

question authority; he is perfectly happy to see someone else shoulder the responsibility. Problems will only arise if you cut a poor figure as leader and the dog feels he should mount a challenge for the top-ranking role.

HOW TO BE A GOOD LEADER

There are a number of guidelines to follow to establish yourself in the role of leader in a way that your Greyhound understands and respects. Greyhounds do not often seek to challenge the status quo, but when your ex-racer comes into your home, he has to learn everything from scratch.

When your Greyhound first arrives in his new home, follow these guidelines:
• **Keep it simple:** Decide on the

rules you want your Greyhound to obey and always make it 100 per cent clear what is acceptable, and what is unacceptable, behaviour.
• **Be consistent:** If you are not consistent about enforcing rules, how can you expect your Greyhound to take you seriously? There is nothing worse than allowing your Greyhound to jump on the sofa one moment and then scolding him the next time he does it because he is muddy. As far as the Greyhound is concerned, he may as well try it on because he cannot predict your reaction. Bear in mind, inconsistency leads to insecurity.
• **Get your timing right:** If you are rewarding your Greyhound

and equally if you are reprimanding him, you must respond within one to two seconds otherwise the dog will not link his behaviour with your reaction (see page XX).

- **Read your dog's body language:** Find out how to read body language and facial expressions (see page XXX) so that you understand your Greyhound's feelings and intentions.

- **Be aware of your own body language:** If your Greyhound is over-awed by his new environment, do not be over-assertive in your behaviour or he will see you as a threat. Instead, help your dog to learn by using your body language to communicate with him. For example, if you want your dog to come to you, open your arms out and look inviting. If you want your dog to stay, use a hand signal (palm flat, facing the dog) so you are effectively 'blocking' his advance.

- **Tone of voice:** Dogs do not speak English; they learn by associating a word with the required action. However, they are very receptive to tone of voice, so you can use your voice to praise your dog or to correct undesirable behaviour. If you are pleased with your Greyhound, praise him to the skies in a warm, happy voice. If you want to stop him raiding the bin, use a deep, stern voice when you say "No".

- **Give one command only:** If you keep repeating a command, or keeping

changing it, your Greyhound will think you are babbling and will probably ignore you. If your Greyhound does not respond the first time you ask, make it simple by using a treat to lure him into position and then you can reward him for a correct response.

- **Daily reminders:** A Greyhound needs constant reminders so he learns how to live in your house and be part of your family. There will be times when he gets it wrong, but rather than coming down on him like a ton of bricks, try to prevent bad manners by

Give one command only so your Greyhound does not become confused.

daily reminders of good manners. For example:

i.   Do not let your dog barge ahead of you when you are going through a door.

ii. Do not let him leap out of the car the moment you open the door (which could be potentially lethal, as well as being disrespectful).

iii. Do not let him eat from your hand when you are at the table.

iv. Do not let him 'win' a toy at the end of a play session and then make off with it. You 'own' his toys and you 'allow' him to play with them. Your Greyhound must learn to give up a toy when you ask.

UNDERSTANDING YOUR GREYHOUND

Body language is an important means of communication between dogs, which they use to make friends, to assert status and to avoid conflict. It is important to get on your dog's wavelength by understanding his body language and reading his facial expressions. This is particularly important with a Greyhound who tends to keep his feelings to himself. This breed has a quiet, deep-thinking temperament, and gives off subtle body language that can easily be missed by people.

• A positive body posture and a wagging tail indicate a happy, confident dog.

• A crouched body posture with ears back and tail down show that a dog is being submissive; a Greyhound may curl his tail right between his legs when he is feeling unsure of a situation. He may also do this when he is being told off or if a more assertive dog approaches him.

• A bold dog will stand tall, looking strong and alert. His ears will be forward and his tail

Learn to read your Greyhound's body language so you can predict his reactions. The black dog is going into a 'play' bow' showing the other dog he is ready for a game.

Some Greyhounds see a game with a toy as the biggest reward.

will be held in line with his body and may swish from side to side.

- A dog who raises his hackles (lifting the fur along his topline) is trying to look as scary as possible.
- A playful dog will go down on his front legs while standing on his hind legs in a bow position. This friendly invitation says: "I'm no threat, let's play."
- A dominant, aggressive dog will meet other dogs with a hard stare. If he is challenged, he may bare his teeth and growl, and the corners of his mouth will be drawn forward. His ears

will be forward and he will appear tense in every muscle.

- A nervous dog will often show aggressive behaviour as a means of self-protection. If threatened, this dog will lower his head and flatten his ears. The corners of his mouth may be drawn back and he may bark or whine.
- Some Greyhounds are 'smilers', curling up their top lip and showing their teeth when they greet people. This should never be confused with a snarl, which would be accompanied by the upright posture of a dominant dog. A smiling dog

will have a low body posture and a wagging tail; he is being submissive and it is a greeting that is often used when low-ranking animals greet high-ranking animals in a pack.

GIVING REWARDS
Why should your Greyhound do as you ask? If you follow the guidelines given above, your Greyhound should respect your authority, but what about the time when he is enjoying a free run across a field? The answer is that you must always be the most interesting, the most attractive and the most irresistible person in

TOP TREATS

Some trainers grade treats depending on what they are asking the dog to do. A dog may get a low-grade treat (such as a piece of dry food) to reward good behaviour on a random basis, such as waiting when you open a door or allowing you to examine his teeth. High-grade treats (which may be cooked liver, sausage or cheese) may be reserved for training new exercises, or for use in the park when you want a really good recall, for example.

Whatever type of treat you use, you should remember to subtract it from your Greyhound's daily food ration. Despite his slim-line physique, a Greyhound is still capable of putting on weight. Fat dogs are lethargic, prone to health problems and will almost certainly have a shorter life-expectancy, so reward your Greyhound, but always keep a check on his figure!

You can also reward your Greyhound by stroking him and giving verbal praise.

your Greyhound's eyes. It would be nice to think that you could achieve this by personality alone, but most of us need a little extra help. You need to find out what is the biggest reward for your dog. In most cases, a Greyhound will be motivated to work for a food reward, although some prefer a game with a toy. But whatever reward you use, make sure it is something that your dog really wants.

When you are teaching a dog a new exercise, you should reward your Greyhound frequently. When he knows the exercise or command, reward him randomly so that he keeps on responding to you in a positive manner.

If your Greyhound does something extra special, like responding instantly when you call him back from a free run, make sure he really knows how pleased you are by giving him a handful of treats or having an extra-long game with his toy. If he gets a bonanza reward, he is more likely to come back on future occasions because you have proved to be even more rewarding than his previous activity.

HOW DO DOGS LEARN?

It is not difficult to get inside your Greyhound's head and understand how he learns, as it is not dissimilar to the way we learn. Dogs learn by

conditioning: they find out that specific behaviours produce specific consequences. This is known as operant conditioning or consequence learning. Consequences have to be immediate or clearly linked to the behaviour, as a dog sees the world in terms of action and result. Dogs will quickly learn if an action has a bad consequence or a good consequence.

Dogs also learn by association. This is known as classical conditioning or association learning. It is the type of learning made famous by Pavlov's experiment with dogs. Pavlov presented dogs with food and measured their salivary response

THE CLICKER REVOLUTION

Karen Pryor pioneered the technique of clicker training when she was working with dolphins. It is very much a continuation of Pavlov's work and makes full use of association learning. Karen wanted to mark 'correct' behaviour at the precise moment it happened. She found it was impossible to toss a fish to a dolphin when it was in mid-air, when she wanted to reward it. Her aim was to establish a conditioned response so the dolphin knew that it had performed correctly and a reward would follow.

The solution was the clicker: a small matchbox-shaped training aid, with a metal tongue that makes a click when it is pressed. To begin with, the dolphin had to learn that a click meant that food was coming. The dolphin then learnt that it must 'earn' a click in order to get a reward. Clicker training has been used with many different animals, most particularly with dogs, and it has proved hugely successful. It is a great aid for pet owners and is also widely used by professional trainers who teach highly specialised skills.

BE POSITIVE!

The most effective method of training dogs is to use their ability to learn by consequence and to teach that the behaviour you want produces a good consequence. For example, if you ask your Greyhound to go "Down" and reward him with a treat, he will learn that it is worth his while to sit on command because it will lead to a treat. He is far more likely to repeat the behaviour, and the behaviour will become stronger, because it results in a positive outcome. This method of training is known as positive reinforcement and it generally leads to a happy, co-operative dog that is willing to work and a handler who has fun training their dog.

The opposite approach is negative reinforcement. This is far less effective and often results in a poor relationship between dog and owner. In this method of training, you ask your Greyhound to go "Down" and if he does not respond, you deliver a sharp yank on the training collar or push on his shoulders to force him into position. The dog learns that not responding to your command has a bad consequence and he may be less likely to ignore you in the future. However, it may well have a bad consequence for you, too. A dog that is treated in this way may associate harsh handling with the handler and become aggressive or fearful. Instead of establishing a pattern of willing co-operation, you are establishing a relationship built on coercion.

(how much they drooled). Then he rang a bell just before presenting the food. At first, the dogs did not salivate until the food was presented. But after a while they learnt that the sound of the bell meant that food was coming and so they salivated when they heard the bell. A dog needs to learn the association in order for it to have any meaning. For example, a dog that has never seen a lead before will be completely indifferent to it. A dog that has learnt that a lead means he is going for a walk will get excited the second he sees the lead; he has learnt to associate a lead with a walk.

GETTING STARTED

As you train your Greyhound you will develop your own techniques as you get to know what motivates him. You may decide to get involved with clicker training or you may prefer to go for a simple command-and-reward formula. It does not matter what form of training you use, as long as it is based on positive, reward-based methods.

There are a few important guidelines to bear in mind when you are training your Greyhound:

- Find a training area that is free from distractions, particularly when you are just starting out. Formal training is entirely alien to the Greyhound, so he will lose concentration very easily in the early stages.
- Keep training sessions short so your Greyhound does not become bored or distracted.
- Do not train if you are in a bad mood or if you are on a tight schedule – the training session will be doomed to failure.
- If you are using a toy as a reward, make sure it is only

It does not take a Greyhound long to learn that a "click" means a reward will follow.

available when you are training. In this way it has an added value for your Greyhound.

- If you are using food treats, make sure they are bite-sized and easy to swallow; you don't want to hang about while your Greyhound chews on his treat.
- Do not attempt to train your Greyhound after he has eaten, or soon after returning from exercise. He will either be too full up to care about food treats or too tired to concentrate.
- When you are training, move around your allocated area so that your dog does not think that an exercise can only be performed in one place.
- If your Greyhound is finding an exercise difficult, try not to get frustrated. Go back a step and praise him for his effort. You will probably find he is more successful when you try again at the next training session.
- If a training session is not going well – either because you are in the wrong frame of mind or the dog is not focusing – ask your Greyhound to do something you know he can do. It could be a simple exercise, such as a "Wait" or a "Down", or it could be a trick he enjoys performing, such as giving his paw. You can then reward him with a food treat or a play with his favourite toy, ending the session on a happy, positive note.
- Do not train for too long. You need to end a training session on a high, with your Greyhound wanting more, rather than making him lose interest by asking too much from him.

In the exercises that follow, clicker training is introduced and followed, but all the exercises will work without the use of a clicker.

INTRODUCING A CLICKER

This is easy, and the intelligent Greyhound will learn about the clicker in record time! It can be combined with attention training, which is a very useful tool and can be used on many different occasions.

- Prepare some treats and go to an area that is free from distractions. Allow your Greyhound to wander, and, when he stops to look at you, click and reward by throwing him a treat. This means he will not crowd you, but will go looking for the treat. Repeat a couple of times. If your Greyhound is very easily distracted, you may need to start this exercise with the dog on a lead.

- After a few clicks, your Greyhound will understand that if he hears a click, he will get a treat. He must now learn that he must 'earn' a click. This time, when your Greyhound looks at you, wait a little longer before clicking and then reward him. If your Greyhound is on a lead but responding well, try him off the lead.

- When your Greyhound is working for a click and giving you his attention, you can introduce a cue or command word, such as "Watch". Repeat a few times, using the cue. You now have a Greyhound that understands the clicker and will give you his attention when you ask him to "Watch".

The Greyhound does not find the Sit an easy exercise.

TRAINING EXERCISES

The Greyhound is a very compliant animal – so much so that some owners do not feel the need to introduce formal training exercises. However, a Greyhound is more than capable of taking this on board, and it will certainly make your life easier if you have a dog who will respond readily to basic instructions.

THE SIT

For most breeds, this is the starting point of all training. However, it does not come naturally for a Greyhound to sit on his hindquarters, so there is little point in insisting on it. The most practical application is when you are about to give your Greyhound his food. He can be taught to "Sit" for a fleeting second, and this may well prevent food being spilled if your Greyhound is keen on his grub and tries to get to the bowl before you put it down.

- When you have prepared your Greyhound's meal, hold the bowl just above his nose. As he looks up, he will naturally go into the 'Sit'. As soon as he is in position, reward him by putting the food bowl down.

- Repeat the exercise and when your Greyhound understands what you want, introduce the "Sit" command.

THE DOWN

Work hard at this exercise because a reliable 'Down' is useful in many different situations, and an instant 'Down' can be a lifesaver.

With practice, your Greyhound will go into the Down position on a verbal cue.

- With other breeds, this exercise is usually taught from the 'Sit', but with a Greyhound it will be just as effective to teach it when the dog is standing. Hold a treat just below your Greyhound's nose and slowly lower it towards the ground. The treat acts as a lure and your dog will follow it, first going down on his forequarters and then bringing his hindquarters down as he tries to get the treat.
- Make sure you close your fist around the treat and only reward your Greyhound with the treat when he is in the correct position. If your Greyhound is reluctant to go 'Down', you can apply gentle pressure on his shoulders to encourage him to go into the correct position.
- When your Greyhound is following the treat and going into position, introduce a verbal command.
- Build up this exercise over a period of time, each time waiting a little longer before giving the reward, so the Greyhound learns to stay in the 'Down' position.

THE RECALL

The Recall is an important exercise, even if you plan to limit the amount of free running that your Greyhound is allowed. You will still need to call your Greyhound in from the garden, or call him back to you after a play session in an indoor equestrian centre where he has socialised with other Greyhounds.

To get a reliable Recall requires time and patience – repetition is the key – and make sure you give a tasty food treat *every* time you get a positive response. When your Greyhound gets the

idea of what you want, you can reward on a random basis when he comes in from the garden, saving high-value rewards for when you need to recall your Greyhound from more challenging situations.

- Start by practising in the garden. When your Greyhound is busy exploring, get his attention by calling his name, and, as he runs towards you, introduce the verbal command "Come". Make sure you sound happy and exciting, so your dog wants to come to you. When he responds, give him lots of praise.
- If your Greyhound is slow to respond, try running away a few paces or jumping up and down. It doesn't matter how silly you look, the key issue is to get your dog's attention and then make yourself irresistible!
- In a dog's mind, coming when

The aim is to build up an enthusiastic response to the recall.

called should be regarded as the best fun because he knows he is always going to be rewarded. Never make the mistake of telling your dog off, no matter how slow he is to respond, as you will undo all your previous hard work.

- When you call your Greyhound to you, make sure he comes up close enough to be touched. He must understand that "Come" means that he should come right up to you, otherwise he will think that he can approach and then veer off when it suits him.

RECALL FROM FREE RUN
If you are confident that you have built up a reliable Recall at home, you can try free running your Greyhound. The best place to choose is a well-fenced field so there is no risk of accidents from passing traffic. Your Greyhound should also wear a muzzle; this is not because we do not trust the dog, it should be seen more in the light of a safety net. Some people may be alarmed at the sight of a Greyhound running at full speed towards them, and it also protects your Greyhound if he meets another dog who is not

as well behaved as he is. So, basically, wearing a muzzle should be seen as a public relations exercise, protecting you and your Greyhound from those who have little or no knowledge of the breed.

- When you free run your Greyhound, make sure you have his favourite toy or a pocket full of tasty treats so you can give high-value rewards when he comes back to you.
- Attach a long lead to your Greyhound's collar. Allow him

to walk ahead of you, and then call him back, just as you did when you were practising in the garden. Reward your Greyhound, and give lots of praise for a correct response.

- Now you can progress to using a 16 ft (4.8 m) training line (a lunge line used for horses will work just as well). At this stage, choose an enclosed area that is relatively free from distractions so that you remain in control. Clip the line to your Greyhound's collar and allow him to explore. When he is some distance ahead, call him back to you and reward him. Your Greyhound has learnt to come when called – he is now learning to come back when he is further away from you.

- The first time you let your Greyhound off the lead, change direction so he is always following you, and not the other way round. If he appears distracted when you call him, use his instinct and run. He is sure to run after you, but remember to reward, even if you have had to work a bit harder to get him back.

- When you are ready to allow your Greyhound off-lead for the duration of his walk, make sure you call him and reward him at intervals throughout the walk. Do not allow your dog to free run and only call him back at the end of the walk to clip on his lead. An intelligent Greyhound will soon realise that the Recall means the end of his walk and then end of fun – so who can blame him for not wanting to come back?

The technique you are using for training the Recall is association learning; the more you repeat an exercise and reward the behaviour, the more likely your Greyhound is to repeat it. Remember, repetition is your best friend when you are teaching your dog something new. You can only say that you have a reliable Recall when your dog consistently comes back to you every time you ask.

SECRET WEAPON

You can build up a strong recall by using another form of association learning. Buy a whistle and when you are giving your Greyhound his food, peep on the whistle. You can choose the type of signal you want to give: two short peeps or one long whistle, for example. Within a matter of days, your dog will learn that the sound of the whistle means that food is coming.

Now transfer the lesson outside. Arm yourself with some tasty treats and the whistle. Allow your Greyhound to run free in the garden, and, after a couple of minutes, use the whistle. The dog has already learnt to associate the whistle with food, so he will come towards you.

Immediately reward him with a treat and lots of praise. Repeat the lesson a few times in the garden, so you are confident that your dog is responding before trying it in the park. Make sure you always have some treats in your pocket when you go for a walk and your dog will quickly learn how rewarding it is to come to you.

In most cases you will find your Greyhound is used to walking on a lead.

WALKING ON A LOOSE LEAD

As a racing dog, your Greyhound would have been walked on-lead on a routine basis as part of his exercise regime. As a result, most Greyhounds are happy to walk on a lead, and this is one of the great pleasures of Greyhound ownership. Many owners report small children walking with a Greyhound on lead, and the dog, with natural empathy, walks quietly and calmly, with no risk of pulling the child over (though this is not to be recommended as the risk can never be fully eliminated, no matter how well trained the dog).

However, you may have a Greyhound who has not learned to walk on a lead, or you may feel the need to brush up on his lead-walking manners.

- Start by using a toy or a tasty treat to encourage your Greyhound. Let him follow the treat/toy for a few paces and then reward him.
- Build up the amount of time your Greyhound will walk with you and when he is walking nicely by your side, introduce the verbal command "Heel" or "Close". Give lots of praise when your dog is in the correct position.
- When your Greyhound is walking alongside you, keep focusing his attention on you by using his name and then rewarding him when he looks at you.

- If you are heading somewhere special, such as the park, your Greyhound may try to pull because he is impatient to get there. If this happens, stop, call your dog to you and do not set off again until he is in the correct position. It may take time, but your Greyhound will eventually realise that it is more productive to walk by your side than to pull ahead.

STAYS

This may not be the most exciting exercise, but it is one of the most useful. There are many occasions when you want your Greyhound to stay in position, even if it is only for a few seconds. The classic example is

You can use the "Stay" command if you want your Greyhound to remain in position for an extended period.

when you want your Greyhound to stay in the back of the car until you have clipped on his lead. Some trainers use the verbal command "Stay" when the dog is to stay in position for an extended period of time and "Wait" if the dog is to stay in position for a few seconds until you give the next command. Others trainers use a universal "Stay" to cover all situations. It all comes down to personal preference, and, as long as you are consistent, your dog will understand the command he is given.

- Put your Greyhound in a 'Down' and use a hand signal (flat palm, facing the dog) to show he is to stay in position.

Step a pace away from the dog. Wait a second, step back and reward him.
- Repeat the exercise, gradually increasing the distance you can leave your dog. When you return to your dog's side, praise him quietly and release him with a command, such as "OK".
- Remember to keep your body language very still when you are training this exercise and avoid eye contact with your dog. Work on this exercise over a period of time and you will build up a really reliable 'Stay'.

SOCIALISATION
Your Greyhound is not only becoming a part of your home

and family, he is becoming a member of the community. He needs to be able to live in the outside world, coping calmly with every new situation that comes his way. It is your job to introduce him to as many different experiences as possible and to encourage him to behave in an appropriate manner.

This is important with all breeds, but it is especially important with a retired Greyhound who, in most cases, has led a narrow life, revolving around kennels and the racetrack. The result of this is that your Greyhound will be very well socialised in some respects, such as travelling, grooming, veterinary inspections and living with other

Your Greyhound may have come straight from kennels and will find adapting to a home environment a challenging experience.

Start off with a walk in a quiet residential area.

Greyhounds. He may also be confident in busy environments, tolerating crowds of people and loudspeaker announcements, which mirror life at a racetrack.

However, your Greyhound will also have enormous blanks in his education. He will probably never have been inside a home; he may never have been up stairs, walked on slippery, laminate floors, or heard household sounds, such as the washing machine, the vacuum or the television. The outside world may also hold many unknowns. Your Greyhound may be used to the type of traffic he would encounter at a racetrack, but he may never have heard air brakes on a lorry, he may never have heard or seen a train, and simple obstacles, such as a stile on a country footpath, may baffle him. He will be used to other Greyhounds, but he is unlikely to have met other breeds of dog. Now, for the first time, he has to learn how to interact with a wide of dogs that could range from an intimidating Rottweiler, a Boxer (whose facial expression is inexplicable to most other dogs, let alone a Greyhound), to a tiny Toy dog that look more like a hare that should be chased than a fellow canine.

Some rehoming organisations run fostering schemes so Greyhounds that have just retired from racing start to learn about domestic life before they are found permanent homes. But in many cases, an ex-racer will come straight from kennels. So, when your Greyhound arrives in his new home, socialisation should be your top priority. A Greyhound with a sound temperament will be quick to catch up on his missed education, particularly if you give him confidence so he realises there is nothing to fear when he encounters a new situation.

IDEAS FOR SOCIALISATION
To begin with, you will need to help your Greyhound to settle into his home. Do not swamp your Greyhound with new experiences, but try to give him the chance to find his feet in his own time. When he is feeling confident, he is less likely to worry if he comes across something new. So let him explore the house – or just the downstairs area if this is to be his domain – before exposing him to the various household machines.

If he is alarmed by anything, just give him time and space. Do not force him to confront the vacuum/washing machine if he takes a dislike to it, but simply reward him for coming a little closer to it. Allow him to sniff

the machine and become accustomed to it, and then maybe wait a few days before turning it on. At all times, adopt a calm, commonsense attitude so your Greyhound is given reassurance. Do not make a fuss of him, or he will think there really is something to fear.

When your Greyhound is confident in the home, you can expand your programme of socialisation to the outside world:

- Start by asking visitors to come to the door, wearing different types of clothing – for example, wearing a hat, a long raincoat, or carrying a stick or an umbrella.
- If you do not have children at

When you feel your Greyhound is ready, take him on outings where he will be among lots of different people.

TRAINING CLUBS

You may think there is little need to go to formal training classes with an adult dog, but there are additional benefits to be gained beyond teaching basic obedience. Your Greyhound will have the opportunity to meet dogs of different breeds in a controlled environment, and this will help to broaden his horizons beyond the Greyhound-only world he has been used to. Your Greyhound will also learn to focus on you, despite the distractions of working alongside others dogs, which will improve his general level of responsiveness.

There are lots of training clubs to choose from. Your vet will probably have details of clubs in your area, or you can ask friends who have dogs if they attend a club. Alternatively, use the internet to find out more information. But how do you know if the club is any good?

Before you take your dog, ask if you can go to a class as an observer and find out the following:

- What experience does the instructor(s) have?
- Do they have experience with Greyhounds?
- Is the class well organised and are the dogs reasonably quiet? (A noisy class indicates an unruly atmosphere, which will not be conducive to learning.)
- Are there are a number of classes to suit dogs of different ages and abilities?
- Are positive, reward-based training methods used?
- Does the club train for the Good Citizen Scheme (see page 119)?

If you are not happy with the training club, find another one. An inexperienced instructor who cannot handle a number of dogs in a confined environment can do more harm than good.

A well run training class will give your Greyhound the opportunity to mix with other dogs of sound temperament.

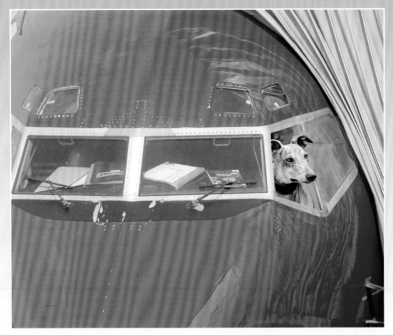

As a Greyhound grows in confidence, you will be amazed at how adaptable he can be.

home, make sure your Greyhound has a chance to meet and play with them. Go to a local park and watch children in the play area. You will not be able to take your Greyhound inside the play area, but he will see children playing and will get used to their shouts of excitement.

- With your Greyhound wearing a muzzle, take a walk around some quiet streets, such as a residential area, to see how your Greyhound reacts to the sound of traffic. When he appears confident, progress to busier areas. Remember, your lead is like a live wire and your feelings will

travel directly to your Greyhound. Assume a calm, confident manner and your dog will take the lead from you and have no reason to be fearful.

- Contact a friend who has a dog of sound temperament so your Greyhound has the chance to meet another breed. Make sure that toys and beds (anything that may encourage territorial behaviour) are put away beforehand. If the dogs get on well, you may be able to make regular dates to exercise them together.
- Go to a railway station. You don't have to get on a train if you don't need to, but your

Greyhound will have the chance to experience trains, people wheeling luggage, loudspeaker announcements and going up and down stairs and over railway bridges.

- If you live in the town, plan a trip to the country. You can enjoy a day out and provide an opportunity for your Greyhound to see livestock, such as sheep, cattle, horses and poultry.
- One of the best places for socialising a dog is at a country fair. There will be crowds of people, livestock in pens, tractors, bouncy castles, fairground rides and food stalls.

It may be that your Greyhound struggles to cope with time on his own.

PROBLEM BEHAVIOUR

In the vast majority of cases, a retired Greyhound will have few problems settling into his new home. Once he feels confident in the home environment, he will take to his new life with remarkable ease, enjoying his creature comforts and thriving on becoming a special dog in a family rather than being one of scores of dogs kept in kennels.

However, there are some Greyhounds that may struggle to make the adjustment, or a dog may be unclear about what constitutes 'appropriate' behaviour in his new home. If you are worried about your Greyhound and feel out of your depth, go back to the rehoming organsiation and ask for help. Most will have a specialist in Greyhound behaviour who will understand the problem and be able to work with you and your Greyhound to find a solution.

SEPARATION ANXIETY

This is probably the most common problem experienced by Greyhounds when they are rehomed. In most cases, it is caused by the Greyhound receiving too much love and attention when he first arrives in his new home. It is easy to see why an owner behaves in this way, and the Greyhound, who has not been used to getting much attention, is more than happy to receive the fuss and cuddles. However, he cannot understand why he is suddenly deprived of this attention when his owner has to go out to work.

Separation anxiety is expressed in a number of ways and all are equally distressing for both dog and owner. An anxious dog who is left alone may bark and whine continuously, urinate and defecate, and may be extremely destructive.

To prevent separation anxiety developing, you should accustom your Greyhound to short periods on his own within the first few days of arriving in your home. He will then accept that temporary absences are a part of his new routine, and he will not become anxious.

If you see signs of separation anxiety, there are a number of steps you can take when attempting to solve the problem:

• Put up a baby-gate between adjoining rooms and leave your Greyhound in one room while you are in the other room. Your dog will be able to see you and hear you, but he is learning to cope without being right next to you. Build up the amount of time you can leave your dog in easy stages.

• Buy some boredom-busting toys and fill them with some tasty treats. Whenever you leave your dog, give him a food-filled toy so that he is busy while you are away.

• If you have not used a crate before, it is not too late to start. Make sure the crate is cosy and train your Greyhound to get used to going in his crate while you are in the same room. Gradually build up the amount of time he spends in the crate and then start leaving

the room for short periods. When you return, do not make a fuss of your dog. Leave him for five or ten minutes before releasing him, so that he gets used to your comings and goings.

• Pretend to go out, putting on your coat and jangling keys, but do not leave the house. An anxious dog often becomes hyped-up by the ritual of leaving and this will help to desensitize him.

• When you go out, leave a radio or a TV on. Some dogs are comforted by hearing voices and background noise when they are left alone.

• Try to make your absences as short as possible when you are first training your dog to accept being on his own.

If you take these steps, your Greyhound should eventually become less anxious, and, over a period of time, you should be able to solve the problem. However, if you are failing to make progress, do not delay in calling in expert help.

RESOURCE GUARDING

During his racing life, a Greyhound will usually share a kennel – in most cases a dog and a bitch are paired together. However, when your Greyhound comes to a new home – and he is the only dog – he will soon realise he has the monopoly on all the comfortable places, such as his dog bed or the sofa if you allow him to lie there. He may have been given toys for the first time, and he may feel he has to

Some Greyhounds get fixated on a toy and resent giving it up.

'guard' these new treasures. He may express this behaviour by growling a warning if you get too close to his bed, if you try to take over his place on the sofa, or if you try to take a toy from him.

In all cases, a Greyhound is showing perfectly natural behaviour – he has found something he values, and he does not want to give it up. But there is a more fundamental, underlying problem. Your Greyhound has failed to recognise you as the leader of his new pack, and he is not giving you the respect this position demands.

If you see signs of your Greyhound behaving in this way, you must work at lowering his status so that he realises that you are the leader and he must accept your authority. Although you need to be firm, you also need to use positive training methods so that your Greyhound is rewarded for the behaviour you want. In this way, his 'correct' behaviour will be strengthened and repeated.

The golden rule is not to become confrontational. The dog will see this as a challenge and may become even more determined not to co-operate. There are a number of steps you can take to lower your Greyhound's status, which are far more likely to have a successful outcome. They include:

- Go back to basics and hold daily training sessions. Make sure you have some really tasty treats, or find a toy your

Greyhound really values and only bring it out at training sessions. Run through all the training exercises you have taught your Greyhound. By giving him things to do, you are giving him mental stimulation and you have the opportunity to make a big fuss of him and reward him when he does well. This will help to reinforce the message that you are the leader and that it is rewarding to do as you ask.

- If your Greyhound does not like you to approach him when he is in his bed, you can turn the tables by making him welcome your presence. Simply drop a few treats near his bed as you walk past. Next time, drop a few treats in the bed. Then call him out of his bed and reward him with a treat.

Tell him to go to his bed, and, after a few minutes, call him to you again. Work at this over a period of time, and your Greyhound will learn that you have control of the bed area, and it is more rewarding to co-operate with you.

- If your Greyhound is becoming possessive over toys, remove all his toys and keep them out of reach. It is then up to you to decide when to produce a toy and to initiate a game. Equally, it is you who will decide when the game is over and when to remove the toy. This teaches your Greyhound that you 'own' his toys. He has fun playing and interacting with you, but the game is over – and the toy is given up – when you say so.
- Sometimes a Greyhound may

try to guard his food bowl. If this happens, put the bowl down empty and drop in a little food at a time. Periodically stop dropping in the food and tell your Greyhound to "Wait". Give it a few seconds and then reward him by dropping in more food. This shows your Greyhound that you are the provider of the food and he can only eat when you allow him to.

- Make sure the family eats before you feed your Greyhound. Some trainers advocate eating in front of the dog (maybe just a few bites from a biscuit) before starting a training session, so the dog appreciates your elevated status.

- Do not let your Greyhound barge through doors ahead of you or leap from the back of the car before you release him. You may need to put your dog on the lead and teach him to "Wait" at doorways and then reward him for letting you go through first.

If your Greyhound is progressing well with his retraining programme, think about getting involved with a dog sport, such as agility. This will give your Greyhound a positive outlet for his energies.

CHASING

The Greyhound's chasing instinct has been discussed earlier (see Chapter Four: Adopting a Greyhound). In the majority of cases, Greyhounds adjust to domestic life, and, with reasonable precautions, chasing small animals is not a problem.

However, there are some Greyhounds that are very keen; this type of dog was probably most successful on the racetrack, and he may struggle to inhibit his chasing behaviour. If a Greyhound has a very strong chase instinct, he will view anything that moves in front of him as something to be chased. This could be small dogs, large dogs, cats, squirrels, rabbits, birds, deer, horses or sheep – even a piece of paper caught by the wind. It is the movement that catches his eye, and his desire is to chase rather than to kill.

The Greyhound's instinct to chase is encouraged and strengthened on the race track.

With hard work and patience you can re-educate your Greyhound and diminish his desire to chase.

With time and patience this type of Greyhound can learn to mix with small dogs, but this will only happen if you understand from the outset that it could take many months of hard work.

When a Greyhound is in the trap at the start of a race, he is unable to look on either side of himself; his head is pointing forwards towards the track. The lure passes by, and it is not until it has reached a certain distance away from the traps that the front of the traps goes up and the dogs sprint out to chase it. This scenario is repeated every time a dog goes racing or schooling. So imagine how a Greyhound will perceive the sight of a small dog

running loose ahead of him in the park. Would you let him off the lead? Certainly not!

The Greyhound will need to have his mind changed from 'to chase' to 'not to chase' if you want him to run off-lead in the company of other dogs. For some Greyhounds their racing mindset may never be changed, but for the majority of Greyhounds, it can be.

To help a Greyhound adjust to the sight of animals running in his view, all attempts by the dog to chase anything must be looked at – from the small dog to a paper bag fluttering in the wind in front of him – both are equally important, as it is the chase

instinct we are trying to help him with, and not the kill, as mentioned before.

With a keen Greyhound, the first few months in his new home are all important. Firstly, consider playtimes. Do not allow your Greyhound to chase after anything – balls, toys, and especially not fluffy toys. Your Greyhound will find it hard to understand what is, and what is not, allowed, so you need adopt a 'can't chase anything' policy, which will help him adjust to his life as a pet.

Your first few trips to the park where there is a strong likelihood of meeting small dogs is going to be difficult for your Greyhound. Do not throw him in at the deep end by immediately letting him mix with other dogs. Instead walk your Greyhound on the perimeter of the park, keeping his head pointing forward. If he looks sideways towards the dogs in the middle of the park, give a gentle nudge with your knee to keep his head pointing forward. This will help him understand that what is going on in the middle has nothing to do with either of you.

Keep these scenarios short and sweet. Do not overload his mind and leave when you feel that your dog is relaxed. Repeat on a daily basis, building up the stimulation day by day until your Greyhound can walk around the perimeter of the park relaxed and looking forwards. This is the first, vital step to helping him change his mindset.

A lot of Greyhound rehoming

AGGRESSION

Aggression is a complex issue, as there are different causes and the behaviour may be triggered by numerous factors. It may be directed towards people, but far more commonly it is directed towards other dogs. Aggression in dogs may be the result of:

- Dominance: This is seen in a dog who is seeking to raise his status in the family pack or among other dogs.
- Defensive behaviour: This may be induced by fear, pain or punishment.
- Territory: A dog may become aggressive if strange dogs or people enter his territory (which is generally seen as the house and garden).
- Intra-sexual issues: This is aggression between sexes – male-to-male or female-to-female.
- Parental instinct: A mother dog may become aggressive if she is protecting her puppies.

The Greyhound is well known for his gentle, laid-back temperament, and aggression is rarely seen in the breed. However, it is important to bear in mind that the Greyhound is a member of the canine race and will show his displeasure, if provoked, in exactly the same way as any dog.

The most common instance of this with a Greyhound is if he is on-lead and other dogs run towards him, invading his personal space. The Greyhound has no place to go, so the only option available is to show aggressive body language in an attempt to inhibit the other dog's behaviour.

Obviously, you will try to steer clear of this type of situation, but if you are concerned that your dog is showing signs of aggressive behaviour that you cannot control, do not delay in calling in expert help.

organisations run desensitising classes to help both owners and Greyhounds alike, so contact your rescue centre to see if they can help you and your Greyhound.

It is very important to keep your Greyhound muzzled when in the presence of other dogs, not only because you will be able to keep your Greyhound under control, but you need to bear in mind that you have no control over other people's dogs that may come running over to yours. This is usually accompanied by a shout from the other dog's owner, saying: "It's OK, he's friendly!" This is of no help whatsoever to you or your Greyhound. Your Greyhound may feel alarmed or confused by the sudden, close presence of a small dog running round his legs. Consider how strange it must be for a Greyhound, who is used to chasing a lure, to suddenly find the lure running around his feet.

Keep close control of all interactions with other dogs, and, above all, be patient, when trying to re-educate your Greyhound.

NEW CHALLENGES

If you enjoy training your Greyhound, you may want to try taking part in some dog-related activities. You can also contact your local rehoming organisation, as many hold fundraising events, which provide a fun day out as well as helping to provide much-needed money for retired Greyhounds.

GOOD CITIZEN SCHEME

This is a scheme run by the Kennel Club in the UK and the American Kennel Club in the USA. The schemes promote responsible ownership and help you to train a well-behaved dog who will fit in with the community. The schemes are excellent for all pet owners and will give your Greyhound the opportunity to mix with other breeds. The KC and the AKC schemes vary in format. In the UK there are three levels: bronze, silver and gold, with each test becoming progressively more demanding. In the AKC scheme there is a single test.

Some of the exercises include:

- Walking on a loose lead among people and other dogs.
- Recall amid distractions.
- A controlled greeting where dogs stay under control while their owners meet.

- The dog allows all-over grooming and handling by his owner, and also accepts being handled by the examiner.
- Stays, with the owner in sight and then out of sight.
- Food manners, allowing the owner to eat without begging and taking a treat on command.
- Sendaway – sending the dog to his bed.

The tests are designed to show the control you have over your dog and his ability to respond correctly and remain calm in all situations. The Good Citizen Scheme is taught at most training clubs. For more information, log on to the Kennel Club or AKC website (see Appendices).

AGILITY

The Greyhound is not your archetypal agility dog – herding types lend themselves better to this discipline – but some Greyhounds are good at it and those that are can give their owners endless enjoyment, plus the opportunity to get and stay fit alongside their dog.

So what is agility? It is a discipline that tests the very foundations of your relationship with your dog. It examines the owner's ability to impart commands and the dog's ability to understand them and act accordingly. To compete in agility, your dog must negotiate an obstacle course that can comprise of:

A Greyhound is more than capable of performing the exercises required in the Good Citizen scheme.

AGILITY COMPETITOR
Greyhounds enjoy the challenge of agility.

Clearing a jump with ease.

Negotiating the weaves.

- Jumps (upright hurdles and long jump)
- Weaves
- A-frame
- Dog walk
- Seesaw
- Tunnels (collapsible and rigid)
- Tyre

Dogs may compete in Jumping classes, with jumps, tunnels and weaves, or in Agility classes, which have the full set of equipment.

Faults are awarded for poles down on the jumps, missed contact points on the A-frame, dog walk and seesaw, and refusals. If a dog takes the wrong course, he is eliminated. The winner is the dog that completes the course in the fastest time with no faults. As you progress up the levels, courses become progressively harder with more twists, turns and changes of direction.

Pedigree and non-pedigree dogs are permitted to compete in this fun sport, which not only provides you with an excellent opportunity to meet new friends and a great way of bonding with your dog, but also has the added bonus of helping you and your Greyhound to stay fit!

GREYHOUND WALKS
This is a relatively new concept: bringing Greyhound lovers together to enjoy one of the greatest and simple pleasures of owning dogs – a stroll in the countryside. It is as simple as that but the enjoyment comes in meeting people with similar interests amid the natural world.

In the UK, Greyhound Walks is based in the east of England. It is a registered charity and aims to improve the socialisation of Greyhounds and Lurchers, promote awareness of Greyhounds as family pets, raise money for local Greyhounds,

Lure coursing is a popular sport in the USA.

and support local Greyhound and Lurcher rehoming schemes.

LURE COURSING

Lure coursing simulates hare coursing using artificial bait dragged across 400-800 metres of countryside. The dogs are released pairs, as in live hare coursing, and compete over a course that is designed to replicate the unpredictability of the course.

Lure coursing has its own set of rules and points-scoring system – just as in live hare coursing – and is another way for you to get greater enjoyment from being the owner of a

Greyhound. On a note of caution, you should be fully aware of your dog's limitations and take veterinary advice should you feel unsure about the fitness of your dog to participate.

This sport is more popular in America and Europe. In the UK, it is conducted through the British Sighthound Organisation. All sighthounds are eligible to compete.

FUN RUNS

Fun runs are becoming increasingly popular, as they present the opportunity for dog and owner to participate in a competitive and healthy pursuit.

Staged mostly for charity, participants in funs runs – owners and dogs – compete over distances between 1 kilometre and 10 kilometres (0.62-6.20 miles). Funs runs are most popular in the US but are being staged more often in Europe and Australia.

DOG SHOWS

A whole new world opens up when you take on a retired Greyhound, including eligibility to enter the hundreds of events that the respective homing organisations arrange through the year, including the opportunity to take part in

If you want to exhibit your Greyhound in the ring, you will need a dog that is bred from show lines

many, many dog shows.

We all have a great deal of pride in our dogs and what better way to have that boosted even further than to take part in a show, and hopefully win or get placed? Information on shows can be obtained through your respective club.

However, you might care to take part in Companion Dog Shows. These are organised in conjunction with the UK Kennel Club and are usually tied in with charity shows. It is not mandatory for your dog to be a pedigree – not an issue for Greyhound owners anyway – to participate, but you, as the dog's owner, must be a member of the Companion Dog Club.

Showing dogs at this level is a whole lot of fun and is not taken too seriously by those who take part. However, if you get bitten by the showing bug, you may want to progress to the top level in the hope that your Greyhound will become a Champion. If this appeals to you, you will need to have a Greyhound that matches the Breed Standard as closely as possible (see Chapter Two: The Perfect Greyhound), and for this you will need to go to a breeder that specialises in producing Greyhounds for the show ring.

SUMMING UP
Whatever you decide to do with your Greyhound, you can rest assured that there is one role in which he will always excel – that of outstanding companion dog.

The Greyhound was a dog that was bred to race, but many owners of retired racing Greyhounds would agree that he seems to find true fulfilment in a family home. Make sure you keep your half of the bargain: spend time socialising and training your Greyhound so that you can be proud to take him anywhere and he will always be a credit to you.

HEALTH CARE

Chapter 8

The retired racing Greyhound is renowned as a faithful companion and a willing friend on a non-conditional basis. He will, however, of necessity rely on you for food and shelter, accident prevention and medication. A healthy Greyhound is a happy chap, looking to please his owner.

There are a few genetic conditions recognised in the Greyhound, which will be covered in depth later in the chapter.

VACCINATION

There is much debate over the issue of vaccination at the moment. The timing of the final part of the initial vaccination course for a puppy and the frequency of subsequent booster vaccinations are both under scrutiny. An evaluation of the relative risk for each disease plays a part, depending on the local situation.

When you take over ownership of a retired racing Greyhound, you will need to check on his vaccination status. This should be recorded on a vaccination certificate. If health and vaccination records are not available, a full vaccination course may be recommended by your vet.

Many owners think that the actual vaccination is the protection, so that their puppy or dog can go out for walks as soon as he or she has had the final part of the vaccination course. This is not the case. The rationale behind vaccination is to stimulate the immune system into producing protective antibodies, which will be triggered if the patient is subsequently exposed to that particular disease. This means that a further one or two weeks will have to pass before an effective level of protection will have developed.

Vaccines against viruses stimulate longer-lasting protection than those against bacteria, whose effect may only persist for a matter of months in some cases. There is also the possibility of an individual failing to mount a full immune response to a vaccination: although the vaccine schedule may have been followed as recommended, that particular dog remains vulnerable.

A dog's level of protection against rabies, as demonstrated by the antibody titre in a blood sample, is routinely tested in the UK in order to fulfil the requirements of the Pet Travel Scheme (PETS). This is not required at the current time with any other individual diseases in order to gauge the need for booster vaccination or to determine the effect of a course of vaccines; instead, your veterinary surgeon will advise a protocol based upon the vaccines available, local disease prevalence, and the lifestyle of you and your dog.

It is worth remembering that maintaining a fully effective level of immune protection against the disease appropriate to your locale is vital: these are serious diseases, which may result in the death of your dog, and some may have the potential to be passed on to his human family (so-called zoonotic potential for transmission). This is where you will be grateful for your veterinary surgeon's own knowledge and advice.

The American Animal Hospital Association laid down guidance at the end of 2006 for the vaccination of dogs in North America. Core diseases were defined as distemper, adenovirus, parvovirus and rabies. So-called non-core diseases are kennel cough, Lyme disease and leptospirosis. A decision to vaccinate against one or more non-core diseases will be based on an individual's level of risk, determined on lifestyle and where you live in the US.

Do remember, however, that the booster visit to the veterinary surgery is not 'just' for a booster. I am regularly correcting my clients when they announce that they have 'just' brought their pet for a booster. Instead, this appointment is a chance for a full health check and evaluation of how a particular dog is doing. After all, we are all conversant with the adage that a human year is equivalent to seven canine years.

There have been attempts in recent times to reset the scale for two reasons: small breeds live longer than giant breeds, and dogs are living longer than previously. I have seen dogs of 17 and 18 years of age, but to say a dog is 119 or 126 years old is plainly meaningless. It does emphasise the fact, though, that a dog's health can change dramatically over the course of a single year, because dogs age at a far faster rate than humans.

For me as a veterinary surgeon, the booster vaccination visit is a

The booster provides an opportunity for the vet to give your Greyhound a through check-up.

Kennel Cough will spread rapidly among dogs that live together.

challenge: how much can I find of which the owner was unaware, such as rotten teeth or a heart murmur? Even monitoring bodyweight year upon year is of use, because bodyweight can creep up, or down, without an owner realising. Being overweight is unhealthy, but it may take an outsider's remark to make an owner realise that there is a problem. Conversely, a drop in bodyweight may be the only pointer to an underlying problem.

The diseases against which dogs are vaccinated include:

ADENOVIRUS

Canine adenovirus 1 (CAV-1) affects the liver (hepatitis) and is seen within affected dogs as the classic 'blue eye', while CAV-2 is a cause of kennel cough (see later). Vaccines often include both canine adenoviruses.

DISTEMPER

This disease is sometimes called 'hardpad' from the characteristic changes to the pads of the paws. It has a worldwide distribution, but fortunately vaccination has been very effective at reducing its occurrence. It is caused by a virus and affects the respiratory, gastro-intestinal (gut) and nervous systems, so it causes a wide range of illnesses. Fox and urban stray dog populations are most at risk and are usually responsible for local outbreaks.

KENNEL COUGH

Also known as infectious tracheobronchitis, *Bordetella bronchiseptica* is not only a major cause of kennel cough but also a common secondary infection on top of another cause. Being a bacterium, it is susceptible to treatment with appropriate antibiotics, but the immunity

stimulated by the vaccine is therefore short-lived (six to 12 months).

This vaccine is often in a form to be administered down the nostrils in order to stimulate local immunity at the point of entry, so to speak. Do not be alarmed to see your veterinary surgeon using a needle and syringe to draw up the vaccine, because the needle will be replaced with a special plastic introducer, allowing the vaccine to be gently instilled into each nostril. Dogs generally resent being held more than the actual intra-nasal vaccine, and I have learnt that covering the patient's eyes helps greatly.

Kennel cough is, however, rather a catch-all term for any cough spreading within a dog population – not just in kennels, but also between dogs at a training session or breed show,

LEPTOSPIROSIS

This disease is caused by *Leptospira interogans*, a spiral-shaped bacterium. There are several natural variants or serovars. Each is characteristically found in one or more particular host animal species, which then acts as a reservoir, intermittently shedding leptospires in the urine. Infection can also be picked up at mating, via bite wounds, across the placenta, or through eating the carcases of infected animals (such as rats).

A serovar will cause actual clinical disease in an individual when two conditions are fulfilled: the individual is not the natural host species, and is also not immune to that particular serovar.

Leptospirosis is a zoonotic disease, known as Weil's disease in humans, with implications for all those in contact with an affected dog. It is also commonly called rat jaundice, reflecting the rat's important role as a carrier. The UK National Rodent Survey 2003 found a wild brown rat population of 60 million, equivalent at the time to one rat per person. Wherever you live in the UK, rats are endemic, which means that there is as much a risk to the Greyhound living with a family in a town as the Greyhound leading a rural lifestyle.

Signs of illness reflect the organs affected by a particular serovar. In humans, there may be a flu-like illness or a more serious, often life-threatening disorder involving major body organs. The illness in a susceptible dog may be mild, the dog recovering within two to three weeks without treatment but going on to develop long-term liver or kidney disease. In contrast, peracute illness may result in a rapid deterioration and death following an initial malaise and fever. There may also be anorexia, vomiting, diarrhoea, abdominal pain, joint pain, increased thirst and urination rate, jaundice, and ocular changes. Haemorrhage is also a common feature, manifesting as bleeding under the skin, nosebleeds, and the presence of blood in the urine and faeces.

Treatment requires rigorous intravenous fluid therapy to support the kidneys. Being a bacterial infection, it is possible to treat leptospirosis with specific antibiotics, although a prolonged course of several weeks is needed. Strict hygiene and barrier nursing are required in order to avoid onward transmission of the disease.

Annual vaccination is recommended for leptospirosis because the immunity only lasts for a year, unlike the longer immunity associated with vaccines against viruses. There is, however, little or no cross-protection between Leptospira serovars, so vaccination will result in protection against only those serovars included in the particular vaccine used. Additionally, although vaccination against leptospirosis will prevent active disease if an individual is exposed to a serovar included in the vaccine, it cannot prevent that individual from being infected and becoming a carrier in the long-term.

In the UK, vaccines have classically included *L. icterohaemorrhagiae* (rat-adapted serovar) and *L. canicola* (dog-specific serovar). The latter is of especial significance to us humans, since disease will not be apparent in an infected dog but leptospires will be shed intermittently.

The situation in America is less clear-cut. Blanket vaccination against leptospirosis is not considered necessary, because it only occurs in certain areas. There has also been a shift in the serovars implicated in clinical disease, reflecting the effectiveness of vaccination and the migration of wildlife reservoirs carrying different serovars from rural areas, so you must be guided by your veterinarian's knowledge of the local situation.

Lyme disease is still relatively rare in the UK.

or even mixing in the park. Many of these infections may not be *B. bronchiseptica* but other viruses, for which one can only treat symptomatically. Parainfluenza virus is often included in a vaccine programme, as it is a common viral cause of kennel cough.

Kennel cough can seem alarming. There is a persistent cough accompanied by the production of white frothy spittle, which can last for a matter of weeks; during this time the patient is highly infectious to other dogs. I remember when it ran through our five Border Collies – there were white patches of froth on the floor wherever you looked! Other features include sneezing, a runny nose, and eyes sore with conjunctivitis. Fortunately, these infections are generally self-limiting, most dogs recovering without any long-lasting problems, but an elderly dog may be knocked sideways by it, akin to the effects of a common cold on a frail, elderly person.

LYME DISEASE

This is a bacterial infection transmitted by hard ticks. It is restricted to those specific areas of the US where ticks are found, such as the north-eastern states, some southern states, California and the upper Mississippi region. It does also occur in the UK, but at a low level, so vaccination is not routinely offered.

Clinical disease is manifested primarily as limping due to arthritis, but other organs affected include the heart,

PARVOVIRUS (CPV)

Canine parvovirus disease first appeared in the late 1970s, when it was feared that the UK's dog population would be decimated by it because of the lack of immunity in the general canine population. While this was a terrifying possibility at the time, fortunately it did not happen.

There are two forms of the virus (CPV-1, CPV-2) affecting domesticated dogs. It is highly contagious, picked up via the mouth/nose from infected faeces. The incubation period is about five days. CPV-2 causes two types of illness: gastro-enteritis and heart disease in puppies born to unvaccinated dams, both of which often result in death. Infection of puppies under three weeks of age with CPV-1 manifests as diarrhoea, vomiting, difficulty breathing, and fading puppy syndrome. CPV-1 can cause abortion and foetal abnormalities in breeding bitches.

Occurrence is mainly low now, thanks to vaccination, although a recent outbreak in my area did claim the lives of several puppies and dogs. It is also occasionally seen in the elderly unvaccinated dog.

kidneys and nervous system. It is readily treatable with appropriate antibiotics, once diagnosed, but the causal bacterium, *Borrelia burgdorferi*, is not cleared from the body totally and will persist.

Prevention requires both vaccination and tick control, especially as there are other diseases transmitted by ticks. Ticks carrying *B. burgdorferi* will transmit it to humans as well, but an infected dog cannot pass it to a human.

RABIES

This is another zoonotic disease and there are very strict control measures in place. Vaccines were once available in the UK only on an individual basis for dogs being taken abroad. Pets travelling into the UK had to serve six months' compulsory quarantine so that any pet incubating rabies would be identified before release back into the general population. Under the Pet Travel Scheme (PETS), provided certain criteria are met (check the DEFRA website for up-to-date information – www.defra.gov.uk) then dogs can re-enter the UK without being quarantined.

Dogs to be imported into the US have to show that they were vaccinated against rabies at least 30 days previously; otherwise, they have to serve effective internal quarantine for 30 days from the date of vaccination against rabies, in order to ensure they are not incubating rabies. The exception is dogs entering from countries recognised as being rabies-free, in which case it has to be proved that they lived in that country for at least six months beforehand.

PARASITES

A parasite is defined as an organism deriving benefit on a one-way basis from another, the host. It goes without saying that it is not to the parasite's advantage to harm the host to such an extent that the benefit is lost, especially if it results in the death of the host. This means a dog could harbour parasites, internal and/or external, without there being any signs apparent to the owner. Many canine parasites can, however, transfer to humans with variable consequences, so routine preventative treatment is advised against particular parasites.

All puppies should be routinely treated for roundworm.

Just as with vaccination, risk assessment plays a part – for example, there is no need for routine heartworm treatment in the UK (at present), but it is vital in the US and in Mediterranean countries.

ROUNDWORMS (NEMATODES)

These are the spaghetti-like worms that you may have seen passed in faeces or brought up in vomit. Most of the deworming treatments in use today cause the adults roundworms to disintegrate, thankfully, so that treating puppies in particular is not as unpleasant as it used to be!

Most puppies will have a worm burden, mainly of a particular roundworm species (*Toxocara canis*), which reactivates within the dam's tissues during pregnancy and passes to the foetuses developing in the womb. It is therefore important to treat the dam both during and after pregnancy, as well as the puppies.

Professional advice is to continue worming every one to three months. There are roundworm eggs in the environment and, unless you examine your dog's faeces under a microscope on a very regular basis for the presence of roundworm eggs, you will be unaware of your dog having picked up roundworms, unless he should have such a heavy burden that he passes the adults.

It takes a few weeks from the time that a dog swallows a Toxocara canis roundworm egg to himself passing viable eggs (the pre-patent period). These eggs are not immediately infective to other animals, requiring a period of maturation in the environment, which is primarily temperature-dependent and therefore shorter in the summer (as little as two weeks) than in the winter. The eggs can survive in the environment for two years and more.

There are deworming products that are active all the time, which will provide continuous protection when administered as often as directed. Otherwise, treating every month will, in effect, cut in before a dog could theoretically become a source of roundworm eggs to the general population.

It is the risk to human health that is so important: *T. canis* roundworms will migrate within our tissues and cause all manner of problems, not least of which (but fortunately rarely) is blindness. If a dog has roundworms, the eggs also find their way on to his coat where they can be picked up during stroking. Sensible hygiene is therefore important. You should always carefully pick up your dog's faeces and dispose of them appropriately, thereby preventing the maturation of any eggs present in the fresh faeces.

TAPEWORMS (CESTODES)
When considering the general dog population, the primary source of the commonest tapeworm species will be fleas, which can carry the eggs. Most multi-wormers will be active against these tapeworms. They are not a threat to human health, but it is unpleasant to see the wriggly ricegrain tapeworm segments emerging from your dog's back passage while he is lying in front of the fire, and usually when you have guests for dinner!

A tapeworm of significance to human health is *Echinococcus granulosus*, found in a few parts of the UK, mainly in Wales. Man is an intermediate host for this tapeworm, along with sheep, cattle and pigs. Inadvertent ingestion of eggs passed in the faeces of an infected dog is followed by the development of so-called hydatid cysts in major organs, such as the lungs and liver, necessitating surgical removal. Dogs become infected through eating raw meat

HEARTWORM (DIROFILARIA IMMITIS)

Heartworm infection has been diagnosed in dogs all over the world. There are two prerequisites: the presence of mosquitoes, and a warm, humid climate.

When a female mosquito bites an infected animal, it acquires D. immitis in its circulating form, as microfilariae. A warm environmental temperature is needed for these microfilariae to develop into the infective third-stage larvae (L3) within the mosquitoes, the so-called intermediate host. L3 larvae are then transmitted by the mosquito when it next bites a dog. Therefore, while heartworm infection is found in all parts of the United States, it is at differing levels. An occurrence in Alaska, for example, is probably a reflection of a visiting dog having previously picked up the infection elsewhere.

Heartworm infection is not currently a problem in the UK, except for those dogs contracting it while abroad without suitable preventative treatment. Global warming and its effect on the UK's climate, however, could change that.

It is a potentially life-threatening condition, with dogs of all breeds and ages being susceptible without preventative treatment. The larvae can grow to 14 inches within the right side of the heart, causing primarily signs of heart failure and ultimately liver and kidney damage. It can be treated but prevention is a better plan. In the US, regular blood tests for the presence of infection are advised, coupled with appropriate preventative measures, so I would advise liaison with your veterinary surgeon.

For dogs travelling to heartworm-endemic areas of the EU, such as the Mediterranean coast, preventative treatment should be started before leaving the UK and maintained during the visit. Again, this is best arranged with your veterinary surgeon.

containing hydatid cysts. Cooking will kill hydatid cysts, so avoid feeding raw meat and offal in areas of high risk.

There are specific requirements for treatment with praziquantel within 24 to 48 hours of return into the UK under the PETS. This is to prevent the introduction of *Echinococcus multilocularis*, a tapeworm carried by foxes on mainland Europe, which is transmissible to humans, causing serious or even fatal liver disease.

FLEAS

There are several species of flea, which are not host-specific. A dog can be carrying cat and human fleas as well as dog fleas, but the same flea treatment will kill and/or control them all. It is also accepted that environmental control is a vital part of a flea control programme. This is because the adult flea is only on the animal for as long as it takes to have a blood meal and to breed; the remainder of the life cycle occurs in the house, car, caravan, shed…

There is a vast array of flea control products available, with various routes of administration: collar, powder, spray, 'spot-on', or oral. Flea control needs to be applied to all pets in the house, regardless of whether they leave the house, since fleas can be introduced into the home by other pets and their human owners. Discuss your specific flea control needs with your veterinary surgeon.

MITES

There are five types of mite that can affect dogs:

(i) **Demodex canis:** This mite is a normal inhabitant of canine hair follicles, passed from the bitch to her pups as they suckle. The development of actual skin disease or demodicosis depends on the individual. It is seen frequently around the time of puberty and after a bitch's first season, associated with hormonal changes.

The localised form consists of areas of fur loss without itchiness, generally around the face and on the forelimbs, and 90 per cent will recover without treatment. The other 10 per cent develop the juvenile-onset

generalised form, of which half will recover spontaneously. The other half may be depressed, go off their food, and show signs of itchiness due to secondary bacterial skin infections.

Treatment may be prolonged over several months and consists of regular bathing with a specific miticidal shampoo. There is also now a licensed 'spot-on' preparation available.

(ii) **Sarcoptes scabei:** This characteristically causes an intense itchiness in the affected Greyhound, causing him to incessantly scratch and bite at himself, leading to marked fur loss and skin trauma. Initially starting on the elbows, earflaps and

Excessive scratching and rolling may be a sign of skin irritation.

hocks, without treatment the skin on the rest of the body can become affected. Fortunately, there is now a highly effective 'spot-on' treatment for *Sarcoptes scabei*.

(iii) ***Cheyletiella yasguri***: This is the fur mite most commonly found on dogs. It is often called 'walking dandruff' because it can be possible to see collections of the small white mite moving about over the skin surface. There is excessive scale and dandruff formation, and mild itchiness. It is transmissible to humans, causing a pruritic rash.

Treatment is with an appropriate insecticide, as advised by your vet.

(iv) ***Otodectes cynotis***: A highly transmissible otitis externa (outer ear infection) results from the presence in the outer ear canal of this ear mite, characterised by exuberant production of dark earwax.

The patient will frequently shake his head and rub at the ear(s) affected. The mites can also spread on to the skin adjacent to the opening of the external ear canal, and may transfer elsewhere, such as to the paws.

Treatment options include specific eardrops acting against both the mite and any secondary infections present in the auditory canal, and certain 'spot-on' formulations.

(v) ***(Neo-) Trombicula autumnalis***: The free-living harvest mite can cause an intense local irritation on the skin. Its larvae are picked up from undergrowth, so they are characteristically found as a bright orange patch on the web of skin between the digits of the paws.

Treatment depends on identifying and avoiding hotspots for picking up harvest mites, if possible. Insecticides can also be applied – be guided by your veterinary surgeon.

TICKS

Ticks have become an increasing problem in recent years

Keep a check on your Greyhound's ears as the presence of mites will cause intense irritation.

throughout Britain. Their physical presence causes irritation, but it is their potential to spread disease that causes concern. A tick will transmit any infection previously contracted while feeding on an animal: for example, Borrelia burgdorferi, the causal agent of Lyme disease (see page 130).

Removing a tick is simple – provided your dog will stay still. The important rule is to twist gently so that the tick is persuaded to let go with its mouthparts. Grasp the body of the tick as near to your dog's skin as possible, either between thumb and fingers or with a specific tick-removing instrument, and then rotate in one direction until the tick comes away. I keep a plastic tick hook in my wallet at all times.

A-Z OF COMMON AILMENTS

ANAL SACS, IMPACTED

The anal sacs lie on either side of the anus at approximately four and eight o'clock, if compared with the face of a clock. They fill with a particularly pungent fluid, which is emptied on to the faeces as they move past the sacs to exit from the anus. Theories abound as to why these sacs should become impacted periodically and seemingly more so in some dogs than others.

The irritation of impacted anal sacs is often seen as 'scooting', when the backside is dragged along the ground. Some dogs will also gnaw at their back feet or over the rump.

Increasing the fibre content of the diet helps some dogs; in others, there is underlying skin disease. It may be a one-off occurrence for no apparent reason. Sometimes an infection can become established, requiring antibiotic therapy,

EAR INFECTIONS

The dog has a long external ear canal, initially vertical then horizontal, leading to the eardrum, which protects the middle ear. If your Greyhound is shaking his head, then his ears will need to be inspected with an auroscope by a veterinary surgeon in order to identify any cause, and to ensure the eardrum is intact. A sample may be taken from the canal to be examined under the microscope and cultured, to identify causal agents before prescribing appropriate eardrops containing antibiotic, antifungal agent and/or steroid. Predisposing causes of otitis externa or infection in the external ear canal include:

- Presence of a foreign body, such as a grass awn
- Ear mites, which are intensely irritating to the dog and stimulate the production of brown wax, predisposing to infection
- Previous infections, causing the canal's lining to thicken, narrowing the canal and reducing ventilation
- Swimming – rarely, because few Greyhounds swim, water can become trapped in the external ear canal and lead to infection, especially if the water is not clean. Likewise, take care around the ears if you have to wash your Greyhound.

The responsible owner should acquire a basic knowledge of the more common canine ailments.

which may need to be coupled with flushing out the infected sac under sedation or general anaesthesia. More rarely, a dog will present with an apparently acute-onset anal sac abscess, which is incredibly painful.

DIARRHOEA

Cause and treatment much as Gastritis (see page 136).

FOREIGN BODIES

- **Internal:** Items swallowed in haste without checking whether they will be digested can cause problems if they

lodge in the stomach or obstruct the intestines, necessitating surgical removal. Acute vomiting is the main sign. Common objects I have seen removed include stones from the garden, peach stones, babies' dummies, golf balls and, once, a lady's bra...

It is possible to diagnose a dog with an intestinal obstruction across a waiting room from a particularly 'tucked-up' stance and pained facial expression. These patients bounce back from surgery dramatically. A

previously docile and compliant obstructed patient will return for a post-operative check-up and literally bounce into the consulting room.

- **External:** Grass awns are adept at finding their way into orifices such as a nostril, down an ear, and into the soft skin between two digits (toes). Once there, the awn starts a one-way journey due to the direction of its whiskers.

In particular, I remember one occasion when a grass awn migrated from a hindpaw, causing abscesses along the way but not yielding itself up until it eventually erupted through the skin in the groin!

GASTRITIS

This is usually a simple stomach upset, most commonly in response to dietary indiscretion. Scavenging constitutes a change in the diet as much as an abrupt switch in the food being fed by the owner. If you are wanting to change your Greyhound's diet after he comes to live with you, it would be a good idea to let him settle in on his original diet before gradually substituting more and more of the diet you want him to eat.

There are also some specific infections causing more severe gastritis/enteritis, which will require treatment from a veterinary surgeon (see also Canine Parvovirus under 'Vaccination' on page 125).

Generally, a day without food, followed by a few days of small, frequent meals of a bland diet (such as cooked chicken or fish), or an appropriate prescription diet, should allow the stomach to settle. It is vital to ensure the patient is drinking and retaining sufficient water to cover losses resulting from the stomach upset in addition to the normal losses to be expected when healthy. Oral rehydration fluid may not be very appetising for the patient, in which case cooled boiled water should be offered. Fluids should initially be offered in small but frequent amounts to avoid over-drinking,

If you exercise your Greyhound in long grass, check him on returning home as grass awns can cause major problems.

which can result in further vomiting and thereby dehydration and electrolyte imbalances. It is also important to wean the patient back on to routine food gradually or else another bout of gastritis may occur.

JOINT PROBLEMS

It is not unusual for older Greyhounds to be stiff after exercise, particularly in cold weather. This is not really surprising for dogs who used to race around a track at high speed. Injuries picked up whilst racing are a common reason for retirement. The Greyhound is such a game breed that a nine- or ten-year-old will not readily forego an extra walk or take kindly to turning for home earlier than usual.

Your veterinary surgeon will be able to advise you on ways of helping your dog cope with stiffness, one of the most important of which will be to ensure that he is not overweight. Arthritic joints do not need to be burdened with extra bodyweight!

LUMPS & BUMPS

Regularly handling and stroking your dog will enable the early detection of lumps and bumps. These may be due to infection (abscess), bruising, multiplication of particular cells from within the body, or even an external parasite (tick). If you are worried about any lump you find, have it checked by a veterinary surgeon.

OBESITY

Being overweight does predispose to many other problems, such as diabetes mellitus, heart disease and joint problems. It is so easily prevented by simply acting as your Greyhound's conscience. Ignore pleading eyes and feed according to your dog's waistline. The body

As your Greyhound gets older you may notice some stiffness, particularly after exercise.

Regular exercise combined with a well balanced diet will help to prevent obesity.

condition is what matters qualitatively, alongside monitoring that individual's bodyweight as a quantitative measure. The Greyhound should, in my opinion as a health professional, have a waistline and it should be possible to feel the ribs beneath only a slight layer of fat.

Retirement from racing, often coupled with neutering, does not automatically mean that your Greyhound will be overweight. Bodyweight is a balance between energy input (food eaten) and energy output (high when in training and racing, lower when living standard family life). Additionally, spaying (ovario-hysterectomy) does slow down the body's rate of working, castration to a lesser extent, so a neutered retired racing Greyhound needs even less food.

If your Greyhound has not been neutered but you plan to have him castrated or her spayed, then I recommend cutting back a little on the amount of food fed a few weeks beforehand to accustom your Greyhound to less food. With respect to a female, if she looks slightly underweight on the morning of the operation, it will help the veterinary surgeon as well as giving her a little leeway weight-wise afterwards. It is always harder to lose weight after neutering than before, because of this slowing in the body's inherent metabolic rate.

On-going dental care is essential for all retired greyhounds.

as anyone who has had toothache will confirm.

Veterinary dentistry has made huge leaps in recent years, so that it no longer consists of extraction as the treatment of necessity. Good dental health lies in the hands of the owner, starting from the moment the dog comes into your care. Just as we have taken on responsibility for feeding, so we have acquired the task of maintaining good dental and oral hygiene.

In an ideal world, we should brush our dogs' teeth as regularly as our own. This is ideally started from puppyhood. It can be hard to introduce the concept of tooth-brushing to an adult dog who has never experienced this, although it provides the perfect opportunity for close contact and quality time, a chance to build up trust and friendship.

The retired racing Greyhound is a special case when it comes to dental health. Preparation for adoption will commonly include dentistry because of dental disease, reflecting the nature and type of racing diet, and the effects of muzzling. Genetic factors may also be involved. Ongoing home-care is vital because plaque will start to accumulate as soon as the first meal is eaten after a dental visit. If plaque is not removed, it calcifies as calculus, predisposing to gingivitis or inflammation of the gums. This is still reversible, but if it is left untreated then more widespread

SKIN SPECIAL NEEDS

A Greyhound's skin is very thin, so they are prone to cuts and gashes. The tail, being long and 'whippy', is also prone to injury and will need protection for a long time while healing; plastic syringe cases have been used successfully, and specific tail splints are now available.

TEETH PROBLEMS

Eating food starts with the canine teeth gripping and killing prey in the wild, incisor teeth biting off

pieces of food and the molar teeth chewing it. To be able to eat is vital for life, yet the actual health of the teeth is often overlooked: unhealthy teeth can predispose to disease, and not just by reducing the ability to eat. The presence of infection within the mouth can lead to bacteria entering the bloodstream and then filtering out at major organs, with the potential for serious consequences. That is not to forget that simply having dental pain can affect a dog's wellbeing, inflammation or periodontal disease can develop, which is not reversible and can have distant effects on the heart, kidneys and liver, as well as causing bad breath, bleeding gums, tooth loss and oral pain.

Fortunately, there are alternative strategies if your Greyhound will not accept having his teeth brushed, ranging from dental chewsticks to specially formulated foods. Regularly checking your dog's mouth and teeth is certainly advisable.

INHERITED DISORDERS

Any individual, dog or human, may have an inherited disorder by virtue of the genes acquired from the parents. This is significant not only for the health of that individual but also because of the potential for transmitting the disorder on to that individual's offspring and to subsequent generations, depending on the mode of inheritance.

There are control schemes in place for some inherited disorders. In the US, for example, the Canine Eye Registration Foundation (CERF) was set up by dog breeders concerned about heritable eye disease, and provides a database of dogs who have been examined by diplomates of the American College of Veterinary Ophthalmologists.

The racing Greyhound is predisposed to certain orthopaedic conditions from the nature of racing around a track. The breed also has several

We are fortunate that the Greyhound suffers from relatively few inherited disorders.

physiological quirks, such as lower red blood cell and platelet counts and a lower level of thyroid hormones than other breeds, whilst blood volume and cardiac output tend to be higher. To date, only a few conditions have been confirmed in the Greyhound as being hereditary. In alphabetical order, these include:

BLOOD-CLOTTING DISORDERS
Type 1 von Willebrand's disease and haemophilia A have been reported in the Greyhound.

CONGENITAL OR SENSORINEURAL DEAFNESS
There is an association with the piebald gene and an increased proportion of white coat colouring. After initially normal development, hearing starts to be

lost from four weeks of age. It is now possible to assess a puppy's hearing accurately from the age of five weeks, using the Brainstem Auditory Evoked Response test.

OSTEOSARCOMA
Studies indicate an increased incidence of neoplasia affecting the bones of the forelimbs, less commonly the femur, of the middle-aged Greyhound. Metastasis (the spread of cancer to other sites) is common, most often to the lungs.

PANNUS (CHRONIC SUPERFICIAL KERATITIS)
This is an inflammatory condition of the outer layer or cornea of the eye, manifesting at two to five years of age. Initially, there is greying of the cornea (which is usually transparent),

then blood vessels and pigment cells migrate across the cornea, reducing vision. It does not seem to be painful. It can be controlled with anti-inflammatory eye drops. It is thought to be inherited in an autosomal recessive fashion,

PROGRESSIVE RETINAL ATROPHY

Starting from around one year of age, this can progress rapidly to total blindness within a year. Inheritance is thought to be autosomal recessive.

SKIN CONDITIONS

Cutaneous asthenia or Ehler-Danlos syndrome: This rare set of disorders arises from inherited defects in the body's fibrous connective tissue (collagen), resulting in unusually stretchy skin that is very susceptible to tearing, e.g. when an affected dog scratches himself. There is usually little bleeding. Small tears will heal readily, leaving white scars, but the tears can enlarge, so early suturing may be necessary. Management involves avoiding trauma by padding corners on furniture and exercising in open spaces, for example. The joints and eyes may also be affected. It is diagnosed from the history and appearance of the skin with multiple scars, and by examination of a skin biopsy.

Idiopathic cutaneous and renal glomerular vasculopathy: Signs may become apparent from as young as six months, up to around five years of age. The hocks, stifles and inner thighs become swollen and tender. Sometimes the forelimbs are also affected. Deep ulceration may occur, and some Greyhounds go on to develop kidney disease, which may be fatal. The mode of inheritance for this disorder has not been identified. It is diagnosed through examination of skin biopsies.

Pattern baldness: Primarily affecting bitches, there is fur loss from the temples and from the underside of the neck, chest and abdomen. There is no discomfort and the remaining coat is normal. Once diagnosed, by excluding other causes of fur loss, there is no treatment available to reverse the baldness.

COMPLEMENTARY THERAPIES

Just as for human health, I do believe that there is a place for alternative therapies alongside and complementing orthodox treatment under the supervision of a veterinary surgeon. That is why 'complementary therapies' is a better name.

Because animals do not have a choice, there are measures in place to safeguard their wellbeing

Increasingly owners are becoming aware of the benefit of complementary therapies.

and welfare. All manipulative treatment must be under the direction of a veterinary surgeon who has examined the patient and diagnosed the condition that he or she feels needs that form of treatment. This covers physiotherapy, chiropractic, osteopathy and swimming therapy. For example, dogs with arthritis who cannot exercise as freely as they were accustomed will enjoy the sensation of controlled non-weight-bearing exercise in water, and will benefit with improved muscling and overall fitness.

All other complementary therapies, such as acupuncture, homoeopathy and aromatherapy, can only be carried out by veterinary surgeons who have been trained in that particular field. Acupuncture is mainly used in dogs for pain relief, often to good effect. The needles look more alarming to the owner, but they are very fine and are well tolerated by most canine patients. Speaking personally, superficial needling is not unpleasant and does help with pain relief. Homoeopathy has had a mixed press in recent years. It is based on the concept of treating like with like. Additionally, a homoeopathic remedy is said to become more powerful the more it is diluted.

SUMMARY

As the owner of a Greyhound, you are responsible for his care and health. Not only must you make decisions on his behalf, you are also responsible for establishing a lifestyle for him that will ensure he leads a long and happy life. Diet plays an important part in this, as does exercise.

For the domestic dog, it is only in recent years that the need has been recognised for changing the diet to suit the dog as he grows, matures and then enters his twilight years. So-called life-stage diets try to match the nutritional needs of the dog as he progresses through life.

An adult dog food or resting Greyhound food will suit the Greyhound living a standard family life. There are also foods for those dogs tactfully termed as obese-prone, such as those who have been neutered or are less active than others, or who simply like their food. Do remember, though, that ultimately you are in control of your Greyhound's diet, unless he is able to profit from scavenging!

On the other hand, prescription diets are of necessity fed under the supervision of a veterinary surgeon because each is formulated to meet the very specific needs of a particular health condition. Should a prescription diet be fed to a healthy dog, or to a dog with a different illness, there could be adverse effects.

It is important to remember that your Greyhound has no choice. As his owner, you are responsible for any decision made, so it must be as informed a decision as possible. Always speak to your veterinary surgeon if you have any worries about your Greyhound. He is not just a dog: from the moment you brought him home, he became a member of the family.

With good care and management, your Greyhound should live a long, happy and healthy life.

THE CONTRIBUTORS

THE EDITOR:
MARK SULLIVAN

Mark Sullivan has been involved with Greyhounds in one way or another for more than 40 years. He has been a breeder, rearer, trainer, racing administrator, reporter on Greyhound sport for both *The Racing Post* and *The Sporting LIfe* and currently runs the popular online shop, Greyhound Megastore as well as broadcasting for Ladbrokes and William Hill.

Mark was the youngest professional greyhound trainer in the late Seventies and in 1981 he trained Summerhill Fun to reach the semi-finals of the English Greyhound Derby. The highlight of his career as a reporter/tipster came in 1990 when he secured a place in the *Guinness Book of World Records* for predicting correctly the winners of all 12 races at a meeting at Wimbledon. Mark is a father of three daughters and also has a granddaughter.

JULIA BARNES

Julia has owned and trained a number of different dog breeds, and has also worked as a puppy socialiser for Dogs for the Disabled. A former journalist, she has written many books, including several on dog training and behaviour. Julia is greatly indebted to Sandra Morris for her specialist knowledge about Greyhounds.
See Chapter Six: Training and Socialisation.

SANDRA MORRIS

Sandra works as an animal behaviourist, and for the last 10 years she has devoted much of her time to helping new owners with their Greyhounds. She visits he owners in their own homes where she can see the Greyhound in his natural environment and watch how both the owners and dog interact with each other. She teaches the owners the basics of the canine language so the dog can understand what their owner is asking of them, and helps them to overcome any problems they may encounter.

For two years, Sandra was chair person of Greyhound Rescue, Wales, and is now concentrating on rescue, rehabilitation and rehoming Greyhounds, working alongside a small team of volunteers.
See Chapter Six: Training and Socialisation.

ALISON LOGAN MA VetMB MRCVS

Alison qualified as a veterinary surgeon from Cambridge University in 1989, having been brought up surrounded by all manner of animals and birds in the north Essex countryside. She has been in practice in her home town ever since, living with her husband, two children and Labrador Retriever Pippin.

She contributes on a regular basis to *Veterinary Times, Veterinary Nurse Times, Dogs Today, Cat World* and *Pet Patter*, the PetPlan newsletter. In 1995, Alison won the Univet Literary Award with an article on Cushing's Disease, and she won it again (as the Vetoquinol Literary Award) in 2002, writing about common conditions in the Shar-Pei.
See Chapter Eight: Happy and Healthy.

USEFUL ADDRESSES

KENNEL & BREED CLUBS

UK
The Kennel Club
1 Clarges Street, London, W1J 8AB
Tel: 0870 606 6750
Web: www.the-kennel-club.org.uk

Greyhound Club
For up-to-date contact information,
please contact the Kennel Club.

USA
American Kennel Club (AKC)
5580 Centerview Drive,
Raleigh, NC 27606, USA.
Tel: 919 233 9767
Email: info@akc.org
Web: www.akc.org

United Kennel Club (UKC)
100 E Kilgore Rd, Kalamazoo,
MI 49002-5584, USA.
Tel: 269 343 9020
Web:www.ukcdogs.com/

Greyhound Club of America
For contact details of regional clubs,
please contact the Greyhound Club of
America.
www.greyhoundclubofamerica.org/

AUSTRALIA
**Australian National Kennel Council
(ANKC)**
The Australian National Kennel
Council is the administrative body for
pure breed canine affairs in Australia. It
does not, however, deal directly with
dog exhibitors, breeders or judges. For
information pertaining to breeders,
clubs or shows, please contact the
relevant State or Territory Controlling
Body.

Dogs Australian Capital Territory
Tel: (02) 6241 4404
Web: www.dogsact.org.au

Dogs New South Wales
Tel: (02) 9834 3022
Web: www.dogsnsw.org.au

Dogs Northern Territory
Tel: (08) 8984 3570
Web: www.dogsnt.com.au

Dogs Queensland
Tel: (07) 3252 2661
Web: www.dogsqueensland.org.au

Dogs South Australia
Tel: (08) 8349 4797
Web: www.dogssa.com.au

Tasmanian Canine Association Inc
Tel: (03) 6272 9443
Web: www.tasdogs.com

Dogs Victoria
Tel: (03)9788 2500
Web: www.dogsvictoria.org.au

Dogs Western Australia
Tel: (08) 9455 1188
Web: www.dogswest.com

INTERNATIONAL
**Fédération Cynologique
Internationalé (FCI)/World Canine
Organisation**
Place Albert 1er, 13, B-6530 Thuin,
Belgium.
Tel: +32 71 59.12.38
Web: www.fci.be/

RESCUE ORGANISATIONS

UK
Retired Greyhound Trust
http://www.retiredgreyhounds.co.uk/

UK Greyhound Rescue Groups
http://www.greyhoundrescue.co.uk/

USA
**National Greyhound Adoption
Program**
www.ngap.org

Greyhound Pets of America
www.greyhoundpets.org/

AUSTRALIA
Each State has its own Greyhound
rescue organisation/s. Please contact
the relevant State authority for details.

OFFICIAL BODIES

UK
**Greyhound Board of Great Britain –
Greyhound Racing**
www.thedogs.co.uk/

Irish Greyhound Board
www.igb.ie

**National Greyhound Racing Club
(NGRC)**
www.ngrc.org.uk/

USA
**Greyhound Racing Association of
America**
www.gra-america.org/

AUSTRALIA
Each State has its own Greyhound
Racing organisation/s. Please contact
the relevant State authority for details.

INTERNATIONAL
Racing Greyhound Information
www.greyhound-data.com

TRAINING AND BEHAVIOUR

UK
Association of Pet Dog Trainers
Web: http://www.apdt.co.uk

Association of Pet Behaviour Counsellors
Web: http://www.apbc.org.uk/

USA
Association of Pet Dog Trainers
Web: www.apdt.com/

American College of Veterinary Behaviorists
Web: http://dacvb.org/

American Veterinary Society of Animal Behavior
Web: www.avsabonline.org/

AUSTRALIA
APDT Australia Inc
Web: www.apdt.com.au

Canine Behaviour
For details of regional behaviourists, contact the relevant State or Territory Controlling Body.

ACTIVITIES

UK
Agility Club
http://www.agilityclub.co.uk/

British Flyball Association
Web: http://www.flyball.org.uk/

British Sighthound Field Association – Lure Coursing
www.lurecoursing.org.uk

USA
North American Dog Agility Council
Web: www.nadac.com/

North American Flyball Association, Inc.
Web: www.flyball.org/

American Sight Hound Field Association
www.asfa.org/

AUSTRALIA
Agility Dog Association of Australia
Web: www.adaa.com.au/

NADAC Australia (North American Dog Agility Council - Australian Division)
Web: www.nadacaustralia.com/

Australian Flyball Association
Web: www.flyball.org.au/

Lure Coursing/Sight Hounds Australia
Please contact relevant State authority.

INTERNATIONAL
World Canine Freestyle Organisation
Tel: (718) 332-8336
Web: www.worldcaninefreestyle.org

HEALTH

UK
Alternative Veterinary Medicine Centre
Web: www.alternativevet.org/

British Small Animal Veterinary Association
Web: http://www.bsava.com/

USA
American Holistic Veterinary Medical Association
Web: www.ahvma.org/

American Veterinary Medical Association
Web: www.avma.org

AUSTRALIA
Australian Holistic Vets
Web: www.ahv.com.au/

Australian Small Animal Veterinary Association
Web: www.asava.com.au

ASSISTANCE DOGS

UK
Canine Partners
Web: www.caninepartners.co.uk

Dogs for the Disabled
Web: www.dogsforthedisabled.org

Guide Dogs for the Blind Association
Web: www.guidedogs.org.uk/

Hearing Dogs for Deaf People
Web: www.hearingdogs.org.uk

Pets as Therapy
Web: http://www.petsastherapy.org/

Support Dogs
Web: www.support-dogs.org.uk

USA
Therapy Dogs International
Web: www.tdi-dog.o

Therapy Dogs Inc.
Web: www.therapydogs.com

Delta Society - Pet Partners
Web: www.deltasociety.org

Comfort Caring Canines
Web: www.comfortcaringcanines.org/

AUSTRALIA
AWARE Dogs Australia, Inc
Web: www.awaredogs.org.au/

Delta Society -- Therapy Dogs
Web: www.deltasociety.com.au

Faithful, good-natured male WLTM like-minded family to share his zest for life. Loves animals, children and enjoys most sports.

If only we could give each of our retired greyhounds their own personal ad. But as the RGT re-homes around five thousand dogs a year, it's just not possible.

We always need more people to adopt our dogs, so perhaps you could help? Retired greyhounds are gentle, intelligent animals who have devoted their early years to racing and now need some TLC in a loving family home.

They ask very little in return: regular walks and meals, the odd cuddle and maybe a warm basket by a cosy fire. So if you're looking for a devoted companion to share happy times, look no further.

Call us on **0844 826 8424** or log on to our website: www.retiredgreyhounds.co.uk

Charity No. 269668

FRSB

give with confidence

retired greyhound trust

Retired Greyhound Trust, 2nd Floor, Park House, 1-4 Park Terrace, Worcester **Park**, Surrey KT4 7JZ
greyhounds@retiredgreyhounds.co.uk
www.retiredgreyhounds.co.uk

Over the last 20 years, the National Greyhound Adoption Program has adopted over 7000 former racing greyhounds in Philadelphia, PA. We are an independent, non-profit program that receives no subsidies from the greyhound racing industry. The facility pictured was completed in October 2009 and can house approximately 100 greyhounds in the most comfortable of settings. All of these greyhounds are available for adoption. In addition to our adoption facility, we also provide boarding services and have a state of the art clinic performing 2000 surgical procedures under anesthesia protocol annually. We have our own in-house crematory.

THE MOST SPECTACULAR GREYHOUND KENNEL

Our greyhounds rest in comfortable, stainless-steel runs that have raised floors and are approximately 125cm wide by 201cm deep. Each run contains a raised bed in back so that our greyhounds can sleep in comfort. They also have the option to lay on the soft rubber mat which lines the front portion of the run. Trench drains run under all of the run areas which make it easy to keep the kennel areas clean and smelling nice. All of our dogs get a chance to run outside four times daily and they also enjoy some 'quiet time' when staff and visitors are not permitted to enter the kennel. Our facility is monitored at all times by twenty-four cameras which can be remotely viewed.

National Greyhound NGAP **Adoption Program**

Raised cage bed

Visit Our Website:
www.NGAP.org

Adoption and Boarding available 365 days a year.

Visitors are welcome daily 9:00-10:30am and 2:00-4:00pm.

Store hours are Monday-Friday 9:00am-4:00pm.

Clinic hours are Tuesdays & Fridays 9:30am-3:00pm

National Greyhound Adoption Program
10901 Dutton Road, Philadelphia, PA 19154
Phone: 215-331-7918
Fax: 215.331.1947
info@ngap.org

Kennel hallway

One of 5 kennels

Food preparation area